The Doctrine & Discipline of the African Union First Colored Methodist Protestant Church

I0153544

1

PREPARED FOR PUBLICATION
BY
HISTORIC PUBLISHING
2017

The Doctrine & Discipline of the African Union First Colored Methodist Protestant Church, of the United States of America, or Elsewhere

African Union Methodist Protestant Church (U.S.)

THE
Doctrine & Discipline
OF THE
AFRICAN UNION
FIRST COLORED
METHODIST PROTESTANT CHURCH,

OF THE UNITED STATES OF AMERICA,
OR ELSEWHERE.

SECOND REVISED EDITION.

PUBLISHED BY ORDER OF THE FIRST GENERAL CONFERENCE
OF THE REPRESENTATIVES OF THE AFRICAN
UNION FIRST COLORED METHODIST
PROTESTANT CHURCH, HELD IN THE
CITY OF WILMINGTON, DELAWARE,

On the 25th day of August, A. D., 1866.

*Revised by the General Conference,
September 24th, 1870.*

**WILMINGTON:
HENRY ECKEL, PRINTER,
JOURNAL BUILDING, 510 MARKET ST.
1871.**

LACONIC HISTORY.

We deem it expedient to annex to our Book of Discipline a brief historical sketch of the rise and progress of the African Union and the First Colored Methodist Protestant Church of the United States of America or elsewhere.

The African Union Church was formerly members of the M. E. Church, of Wilmington, Delaware, of African descent, and as early as A. D., 1805; and as the M. E. Church in this region thought proper to deny the colored members of said Church the privileges guaranteed by the word of God and His liberal Gospel, did quietly withdraw from the connection of said Church, and erecting a house of worship, where we could worship God according to the enlightened dictates of our consciences, and for the exercises of our spiritual gifts; and in the prosecution of our undertaking we experienced from the hands of the Lord a peculiar manifestation of Divine favor, and through our own exertions, and the liberality of all the religious denominations, we were able to build a house for religious worship the same year.

Then we thought we could have the rule of our Church so as to make our own rules and laws for ourselves, only we knew that we must help to support the preachers that were stationed in Wilmington to preach at both Churches, which we were willing to do. We then thought we had power to refuse any that were not thought proper persons to preach to us, but the stationed preacher that was in Wilmington to preach, told us plainly that we had no say, and he must be the entire judge of all. Then that body of us who built the meeting house could not see our way clear to give up all say, and for that reason our Minister said that we had broke the Discipline, and turned out all the Trustees and Class Leaders, and never allowed us a hearing. This was done December, 1812, and after many sorrowful times, and among all the rest a small party, the most of them strangers, that knew but little of the cause that we built a house for, they told the Elder they were willing to be governed by the Discipline, and do what he told them, and then things went on worse and worse, till at length we were brought before the Magistrate, and last of all we had to go before the Court, which cost us much loss of time and money. We then saw that if we did not let that Church go, we might look for nothing but lawing, unless we would comply and let the preacher do as he pleased.

For the sake of peace and love, and nothing but that, we soberly came away, and we mean that all shall see all we want is peace. For the sake of peace and love and nothing else, better is a morsel with content, than a house full where there is contention. What is here written is true, and may the Lord lead us by His counsel, and then bring us to glory the way that we are now in. We appeal to Him that knows all things, that the influences by which we was surrounded compelled us to pursue this course for we had no one to direct us but the Lord, and to Him be glory for ever and ever.

We remain your affectionate brethren and pastors, willing to labor night and day for your spiritual good.

PETER SPENCER,
WILLIAM ANDERSON.

Having purchased another place of worship, pursuant to public notice, the members met at their Church, known and distinguished by the name of the Union Church, on the 7th day of September, A. D., 1813, for the purpose of electing Ruling Elders to take charge of their spiritual affairs of the Church.

They did then and there elect suitable brethren for that purpose by plurality vote, and on the 14th day of September, A. D., 1813, the said Elders met and did set apart WILLIAM ANDERSON and PETER SPENCER to be their Preachers, and to perform all the religious services in the said Union Church, proper for Gospel Ministers to do. This body of Christians having experienced severe trials in order to advance the interests of the cause of the Blessed Redeemer, and desirous of being an independent Religious body, did by a Convential Act, create themselves into a body of Christians, to be known and distinguished by the name of the African Union Church, and agreeable to the laws of the State of Delaware, they became a body politic, and are governed by the Articles of the Association in conformity to the Act of Incorporation.

EXTRACT.

"ARTICLES OF ASSOCIATION OF THE AFRICAN UNION CHURCH, IN WILMINGTON, STATE OF DELAWARE.

"ARTICLE I.

"The style and title of this Corporation shall be the 'Union Church,' of African Members, at Wilmington, Delaware, and Scotland Hill, David Smith, Jacob March, Benjamin Webb, John Simmons, John Kelley and Peter Spencer members of the said Church (now duly elected) and their successors duly qualified and elected as hereinafter directed, shall be the Trustees."

Recorded September 18th, 1813.

STATE OF DELAWARE, s. s.
New Castle County, s. s.

I, the undersigned, Recorder of Deeds in and for said County, hereby certify the above and foregoing six pages contain a true copy of the record of a deed recorded in the office for Recording of Deeds, at New Castle, in book M., vol. III, p. 470, &c.

L. S. Witness my hand and seal of said office.

WM. D. OCHELTREE, Recorder.

Per ARTHUR MCCALLMONT.

We cannot dismiss this laconic narrative without saying, that more than a half century has passed since the first blow was struck for religious liberty by those venerable founders of the Church, for whose indefatigable exertions future generations will rise up and call them blessed.

The religious enterprise gave an impetus to the great and glorious cause of Religion, and the different colored bodies of Methodists in the various parts of the United States were induced to swell this noble stream of religious liberty. But it is a source of much regret that difficulties should have occurred among us in relation to Church Government, which caused the First Colored Methodist Protestant Church in the city of Baltimore, State of Maryland, and the Colored Methodist Protestant Church, in the city of Philadelphia, State of Pennsylvania, to withdraw from the A. M E. Church of the United States of America, and by a Conventional Act they were duly organized into a Church, known by the name of the First Colored Methodist Protestant Church.

PREFACE.

We, the representatives of the First Colored Methodist Protestant Churches, in General Convention, June, 1850, assembled, acknowledging the Lord Jesus Christ as the only Head of the Church, and the word of God as the sufficient rule of faith and practice in all things pertaining to Godliness, and being fully persuaded that the Representative form of Church government is the most Scriptural, best suited to our condition, and the most congenial with our views and feelings as fellow-citizens with the saints and of the household of God; and whereas, a written Discipline, establishing the form of Government, and securing to the Minister and the members of Church their rights and privileges, is the best safeguard of Christian liberty; we therefore, trusting in the protection of Almighty God, and acting in the name and by the authority of our constituents, do ordain and establish, and agree to be governed by the following elementary principles of Discipline.

We deem it inexpedient to enlarge upon the causes of our withdrawal from the A. M. E. Church, or to annex the elementary principles of our Discipline, as we intend to publish in pamphlet form an exposition of the whole matter.

In conclusion, we beg leave to state that this branch of the Church of Christ, being duly organized under the fostering care of the "Great Bishop of the Church," and guided by his counsel, firm as a rock the Church shall stand, amidst scenes of confusion and members complaints. The Almighty, who always watches over the destinies of His people, put it into the heart of a brother to suggest a plan to advance the interests of the Church, by uniting two branches of the Christian Church into one inseparable interest, namely : The African Union Church and the First Colored Methodist Protestant Church, and to effect this object a General Convention was called, and due notice given to the different Churches in connection with the two religious bodies.

Pursuant to special notice, the Representatives of the African Union Church, and the First Colored Methodist Protestant, met in General Convention on the afternoon of the 25th day of November, A. D. 1865, at 3 o'clock, in St. Thomas Church, in the city of Baltimore, and after the protracted Session of several days, the Convention adopted a platform to unite the two branches of Zion into one Church. to be known and distinguished by the name of the African Union First Colored Methodist Protestant Church of the United States of America, or elsewhere. And to consummate the union, the General Convention do hereby constitute a General Conference, to consist of an equal number of delegates from each Church, to be held in the city of Wilmington, Delaware, on the morning of the 25th day of August, A. D., 1866.

Pursuant to previous arrangements, the First General Conference of the Representatives of the African Union Church, and the First Colored Methodist Protestant Church, met in General Conference, assembled on the 25th day of August, A. D., 1866, in the city of Wilmington, State of Delaware. The General Conference did then and there form a Book of Discipline for their future government:

AND WHEREAS, We, the Representatives of the African Union First Colored Methodist Protestant Church, in General Conference assembled, acknowledging the Lord Jesus Christ as the only Head of the Church, and the Word of God as the sufficient rule of faith and practice in all things pertaining to Godliness, and being fully persuaded that the representative form of Church government is the most Scriptural, best suited to our condition, and most congenial with our views and feelings as fellow citizens with the Saints, and of the household of God.

AND WHEREAS, A written Discipline, establishing the form of Government and securing to the Ministers and members of the Church their rights and privileges, is the best safeguard of Christian liberty.

We therefore, trusting in the protection of Almighty God, and acting in the name and by the authority of our constituents, do ordain and establish, and agree to be governed by the following articles of Discipline.

ARTICLES OF RELIGION.

THE CREED.

I believe in God the Father Almighty, Creator of Heaven and Earth, and in Jesus Christ, His only Son our Lord, who was conceived by the Holy Ghost, born of the Virgin Mary, suffered under Pontius Pilate, was crucified, dead and buried; the third day he arose from the dead and ascended into Heaven, and sat at the right hand of God the Father Almighty; from thence He shall come to judge the living and the dead. I believe in the Holy Ghost, the Holy Catholic Church, the Communion of Saints, the forgiveness of Sins, Resurrection of the Body and the Life everlasting. Amen.

1. OF FAITH IN THE HOLY TRINITY.

There is but one living and true God, everlasting without body or parts, of infinite power, wisdom and goodness; the maker and preserver of all things visible and invisible; and in unity of this God Head there are three, persons, of one substance, power and eternity: The Father, the Son and the Holy Ghost.

2. OF THE WORD OR SON OF GOD.

The Son, who is the word of the Father, the very and eternal God of one substance with the Father, took man's nature in the womb of the blessed Virgin.

3. OF THE RESURRECTION OF CHRIST.

Christ did truly rise again from the dead and took again His body, with all things appertaining to the perfection of man's nature, wherewith he ascended into Heaven and there sitteth until He returns to judge men at the last day.

4. OF THE HOLY GHOST.

The Holy Ghost proceeding from the Father and the Son, is one of substance, majesty, power and glory with the Father and Son very eternal God.

5. THE SUFFICIENCY OF THE HOLY SCRIPTURES FOR SALVATION.

The Holy Scriptures contain all things necessary to salvation, so that whatsoever is not read therein, nor can be proved thereby, is not to be required of any man that it should be believed as an article of faith, or thought requisite or necessary for salvation. In the name of the Holy Scriptures, we do understand those Canonical Books of the Old and New Testament, of whose authority was never any doubt in the Church.

The names of the Canonical Books:

Genesis, Exodus, Leviticus, Numbers, Deuteronomy, Joshua, Judges, Ruth, the first book of Samuel, the second book of Samuel, the first book of Kings, the second book of Kings, the first book of Chronicles, the second book of Chronicles, the book of Job, the Psalms, the Proverbs of Solomon, Ecclesiastes, or the Preacher, Cantica, or the Song of Solomon, Four Prophets, the greater, Twelve Prophets, the less.

All the Books of the New Testament as they are commonly received, we do receive and number canonical.

6. OF THE OLD TESTAMENT.

The Old Testament is not contrary to the New, for through both Old and New Testament everlasting life is offered to mankind by Christ, who is the only Mediator between God and man, being God and man; wherefore they are not to be heard who feign that the Old Father did not look only for transitory promises, although the law given from God to Moses, as touching ceremonies and rights, doth not bind Christians, nor ought the civil precepts thereof of necessity be received in any commonwealth; yet notwithstanding, no Christian whatsoever is free from the obedience of the commandments which are called moral.

7. OF ORIGINAL OR BIRTH SIN.

Original Sin stands not in the following of Adam, but is the corruption of the nature of every man that naturally is engendered of the offspring of Adam, whereby man is very far gone from original righteousness, and of his own nature inclined to evil, and that continually.

8. OF FREE WILL.

The condition of man is such, after the fall of Adam, that he cannot turn and prepare himself by his own natural strength and works of faith, and calling upon God, wherefore we have no power to do good works, pleasant and acceptable to God, without the grace of God, by Christ on us, that we may have a good will working in us when we have that will.

9. OF THE JUSTIFICATION OF MAN.

We are accounted righteous before God, only for the merit of our Lord and Saviour Jesus Christ, by faith, and not for our works or deservings; wherefore, that we are justified by faith only is a most wholesome doctrine and full of comfort.

10. OF GOOD WORKS.

Although good works, which are the fruits of faith and follow after justification, cannot put away our sins and endure the severity of God's judgment, yet are they pleasing and acceptable to God in Christ, and spring out of a true and lively faith, insomuch that by them a lively faith is known as evidently as a tree is discerned by its fruits.

11. OF WORKS OF SEPEREROGATION.

Voluntary works besides, over and above God's commands, which are called works of supererogation, cannot be taught without arrogance and impiety, for by them men do declare that they not only render unto God as much as they are bound to do, but, that they do more for His sake than of bounded duty is required; whereas Christ saith plainly, when ye have done all that is commanded you ye are unprofitable servants.

12. OF SIN AFTER JUSTIFICATION.

Not every sin willingly committed after justification is the sin against the Holy Ghost, and unpardonable; wherefore the grant of repentance is not to be denied to such as fall into sin after justification. After we have received the Holy Ghost we may depart from grace given and fall into sin, and by the grace of God rise again and amend our lives; and therefore they are to be condemned who say they can no more sin as long as they live here, or deny the place of forgivness to such as truly repent.

13. OF THE CHURCH.

The visible Church of Christ is a congregation of faithful men and women, in which the pure word of God is preached and the sacraments duly administered according to Christ's ordinance, in all those things that of necessity are requisite to the same.

14. OF PURGATORY.

The Romish doctrine concerning purgatory, pardon, worshipping and adoration of images, as well as of relics, and also the invocation of Saints, is a fond thing vainly invented, and grounded upon no warrant of Scripture, but repugnant to the word of God.

15. OF SPEAKING IN THE CONGREGATION IN SUCH A TONGUE AS THE PEOPLE UNDERSTAND.

It is a thing plainly repugnant to the word of God, and to the custom of the primitive Church to have public prayer in the Church or to minister the Sacraments in a tongue not understood by the people.

16. OF THE SACRAMENTS.

Sacraments ordained by Christ are not only badges of Christian men's profession, but rather they are certain signs of grace and God's good-will towards us, by which He doth work invisibly in us, and doth not only quicken, but also strengthens and comforts our faith in Him.

There are only two Sacraments ordained of Christ our Lord, in the gospel; that is to say, Baptism and the Lord's Supper.

Those five commonly called Sacraments, that is to say: Confirmation, Penance, Orders, Matrimony and Extreme Unction, are not to be considered Sacraments of the gospel, such as have partly grown out of the corrupt following of the Apostles, and partly are states of life allowed in the Scripture, but yet have not the like nature of Baptism and the Lord's Supper, because they have not any visible signs of the ceremony ordained by God.

The Sacraments were not ordained by Christ to be gazed upon or to be carried about, but that we should duly use them; and in such only as worthily receive the same, they have a wholesome effect or operation, but they that receive them unworthily purchase to themselves condemnation.

17. OF BAPTISM.

Baptism is not only a sign of profession and a mark of difference, whereby Christians are distinguished from others that are not baptised, but also a sign of regeneration or the new birth. The baptism of children is to be retained in the Church,

18. OF THE LORD'S SUPPER.

The supper of the Lord is not only a sign that Christians ought to have among themselves, one to another, but is rather a sacrament of our redemption by Christ's death, inasmuch that to such as rightly, worthily, and with faith, receive the same; the bread which we break is a partaking of the body of Christ, and likewise the cup of blessing is a partaking of the blood of Christ.

Transubstantiation or the change of the substance of bread and wine in the Supper of our Lord, cannot be proved by Holy Writ, but it is repugnant to the plain words of the Scriptures, overthroweth the nature of a Sacrament, and hath given occasion to many superstitions. The body of Christ is given, taken and eaten, in the Supper, only after a heavenly manner; and the means whereby the body of Christ is received and eaten in the supper is faith.

The Sacraments of the Lord's Supper was not by Christ's ordinance reserved to be carried about, lifted up or worshipped.

It is necessary to state the importance and obligations of frequenting this means of grace. Surely it is enough that Christ himself instituted this holy and distinguishing ordinance of the New Testament at the most affecting and impressive period of His earthly history, and has solemnly enjoined the observance of it upon every member of His church.

"This do ye in remembrance of me, for as often as ye eat this bread and drink this cup, ye do show the Lord's death till He come."

Such are the interesting views given us of this subject in the Sacred
Scriptures, and who can approach the memorials of his Saviour's sufferings and
death, without having his heart deeply penetrated with a sense of the great and
destructive evil of sin, and His faith and hope elevated exclusively to that
Redeemer who was wounded for our transgressions and bruised for our
iniquities. Let us, therefore, beloved brethren, with constancy and holy delight,
honor on all occasions this positive institution of our Divine Master.

19. OF BOTH KINDS

The cup of the Lord is not to be denied to the lay members, for both parts of
the Lord's Supper, by Christ's ordinance and commandments, ought to be
administered to all Christians alike.

20. OF THE ONE OBLATION OF CHRIST, FINISHED UPON THE CROSS

The offering of Christ once made is that perfect redemption, propitiation
and satisfaction, for all the sins of the whole world both original and actual, and
there is none other satisfaction for sin but that alone; therefore the sacrifices of
masses, in which it is commonly said that the priest doth offer Christ for the
quick and the dead, to have remission of guilt or pain, is a blasphemous fable and
dangerous deceit.

21. OF THE MARRIAGE OF MINISTERS.

The Ministers of Christ are not commanded by God's law either to vow the
estate of single life or to abstain from marriage; therefore, it is lawful for them,
as for all Christians, to marry at their own discretion, as they shall judge the
same to be best to Godliness.

22. OF THE RITES AND CEREMONIES OF THE CHURCH.

It is not necessary that rites and ceremonies should in all places be exactly
alike, for they have been always different, and may be changed according to the
diversities of countries, times and men's manners, so that nothing may be
ordained against God's word whatsoever, through his private judgment, willingly
purposely doth openly break the rites and ceremonies of the Church to which he
belongs, which are not repugnant to the word of God and are ordained and

approved by common authority, ought to be rebuked only that others may fear to do the like, as one that offendeth against the common order of the Church, and woundeth the conscience of weak brethren.

Every particular Church may ordain, change or abolish rites and ceremonies, so that all things may be done to edification.

23. OF THE RULES OF THE UNITED STATES OF AMERICA.

The President, the Congress, the General Assemblies, the Governors and Councils of State, as the delegates of the people, are the rulers of the United States, and the said States are a sovereign and independent nation, and ought not to be subject to any foreign jurisdiction.

24. OF CHRISTIAN MEN'S GOODS.

The riches and goods of Christians are not common as touching the right, title and possession of the same, as some do falsely boast; notwithstanding every man ought of such things as he possesseth, liberally give alms to the poor, according to his ability.

25. OF A CHRISTIAN MAN'S OATH.

As we confess that vain and rash swearing is forbidden Christian men by our Lord and Saviour Jesus Christ, and St. James his Apostle, so we judge that the Christian religion doth not prohibit but that a man may swear when the Magistrate requireth, in a cause of faith and charity, so it be done according to the prophets teachings, in justice, judgment and truth.

GENERAL RULES OF ADMISSION.

There is one only condition previously required of those who desire admission into these societies:--a desire to flee the wrath to come, and be saved from their sins. But, whenever this is really fixed in the soul, it will be shown by its fruits. It is therefore expected of all who continue therein, that they evidence a desire of salvation. First, by doing no harm; by avoiding evil of every kind, especially that which is most generally practiced, such as, taking the name of God in vain; profaning the Lord's day, either by doing ordinary work thereon, or buying or selling; drunkenness; buying or selling spirituous liquors, or drinking them, unless in cases of extreme necessity; fighting, quarrelling, brawling; brother going to law with brother; returning evil for evil, or railing for railing. The using of many words in buying or selling; the buying or selling of unaccustomed goods; the giving or taking things on usury, i. e. unlawful interest; uncharitable or unprofitable conversation, particularly speaking evil of Magistrates or Ministers. Doing to others as we would not they should do unto us; doing what we know is not for the glory of God, such as the putting on of gold or costly apparel; the taking such diversions as cannot be used in the name of the Lord Jesus; singing those songs, or reading those books, which do not tend to the knowledge or love of God; needless self-indulgence; laying up treasures upon earth; borrowing without a probability of paying, or taking up goods without a probability of paying for them.

2. It is expected of all who continue in these societies, that they continue to evidence these desires of salvation; secondly, by doing good, by being in every kind merciful after their power, as they have opportunity; doing good of every possible sort, and as far as is possible to all men. To their bodies, of the ability which God giveth, by giving food to the hungry; by clothing the naked; by visiting or helping them that are sick, or in prison. To their souls by instructing, reproving or exhorting all we have any intercourse with; tramping under foot that enthusiastic doctrine of devils, that we are not to do good unless our hearts be free to it.

By doing good especially to them that are of the household of faith, or growing so be, employing them preferably to others; buying one of another; helping each other in business, and so much the more, because the world will love its own, and them only.

By all possible diligence and frugality, that the gospel be not blamed.

By running, with patience, the race that is set before them, denying themselves, and taking up their cross daily; submitting to bear the reproach of Christ; to be as the filth and off scouring of the world, and looking that men should say all manner of evil against them falsely for the Lord's sake.

3. It is expected of all who desire to continue in these societies, that they continue to evidence their desire of salvation. Thirdly, by attending on all the ordinances of God, such are the public worship of God; the ministry of the word, either read or expounded; the supper of the Lord; family and private prayer; searching the scriptures; and fasting or abstinence.

These are the general rules of our societies, all of which we are taught of God to observe, even in His written word; the only rule, and the sufficient rule, both of our faith and practice.

And all these, we know His spirit writes on every truly awakened heart. If there by any among us who observe them, not, who habitually break any of them, let it be made known unto them who watch over those souls, as they that must give an account. We will admonish those for a season, but then, if they repent not, he hath no more place among us, we have delivered our own souls[.]

Questions to be asked those persons coming forward to join church:

Q. Has God for Christ's sake pardoned you of your sins?

Q. And are you determined to serve him the remainder of your days.

Q. Are you willing to comply with the rules and government of our Church?

Q. Are you willing to pay your tithes for the support of the Minister, and the contingent expenses of the Church?

Q. Will you be faithful in attending public and private meeting of the church, and are you willing to be admonished by us when you are found doing wrong?

These questions being answered satisfactorily, the minister shall then say, their being no objection, we take them in on probation for six months.

Persons received from other denominations by letter, whenever present, let the following questions be asked:

How long are you expected to remain with us? Are you willing to be ruled and governed by the Discipline of our Church?

These questions answered satisfactorily they may be taken in in full membership.

DOCTRINE.

1st.--Question 1.--What is it to be justified?

Answer.--To be pardoned and received into God's favor, in such a state, that if we continue therein, we shall be finally saved.

Q. 2.--Is faith the condition of justification?

A.--Yes, for every one that believeth not is condemned, and every one who believes is justified.

Q. 3.--But must not repentance, and works meet for repentance, go before this faith?

A.--Without doubt, if by repentance you mean conviction of sin, and by works meet for repentance, obeying God as far as we can, forgiving our brother, leaving off from evil, doing good and using his ordinances according to the power we have received.

Q. 4.--What is faith?

A.--Faith in general is a divine supernatural elenchos of things not seen, i. e. past, future or spiritual things. It is a spiritual view of God, and the things of God.

First a sinner is convinced by the Holy Ghost, Christ loved me, and gave himself for me. This is that faith by which he is justified or pardoned, the moment he receives it. Immediately the same spirit bears witness, Thou art pardoned, thou hast redemption in his blood! And this is saving faith, whereby the love of God is shed abroad in his heart.

Q, 5.--Have all Christians this faith? May not a man be justified and not know it?

A.--That all true Christians have such a faith as implies assurance of God's love, appears from Rom. viii, 15; Eph. iv, 32; 2 Cor. xiii, 5; Heb. viii, 10; 1 John iv, v. 10. 19. And that no man can be justified and not know it, appears further from the nature of the thing: For faith after repentance, is ease after pain, rest after toil, light after darkness. It appears also from the immediate, as well as distant fruits thereof.

Q. 6.--But may not a man go to heaven without it?

A.--It does not appear from holy writ, that a man who has heard the gospel, can: (Mark xvi. 16) whatever a heathen may do. (Rom. ii, 14.)

Q. 7.--What are the immediate fruits of justifying faith?

A.--Peace, joy, love, power over all outward sin, and power to keep down inward sin.

Q. 8.--Does any one believe who has not the witness in himself, or any longer than he sees, loves, and obeys God?

A.--We apprehend not--*seeing* God being the very essence of faith; love and obedience being the inseparable properties of it.

Q. 9.--What sins are consistent with justifying faith?

A.--No wilful sin. If a beleiver wilfully sins, he casts away his faith. Neither is it possible he should have justifying faith again, without previously repenting.

Q. 10--Must every believer come into a state of doubt or fear or darkness? Will he do so unless by ignorance or unfaithfulness? Does God otherwise withdraw himself?

A.--It is certain a believer need never come again into condemnation. It seems he need not come into a state of doubt or fear, or darknesss, and that (ordinarily at least,) he will not, unless by ignorance or unfaithfulness. Yet it is true, that the first joy seldom lasts long; that it is followed by doubts and fears; and that God frequently permits great heaviness, before any large manifestation of himself.

Q. 11--Are works necessary to the continuance of faith?

A.--Without doubt; for a man may forfeit the free gift of God, either by sins of omission or commission.

Q. 12--Can faith be lost, but for want of works?

A.--It cannot but through disobedience?

Q. 13.--How is faith *made perfect by works?*

A.--The more we exert our faith, the more it is increased. To him that hath, shall be given.

Q, 14--St. Paul says, Abraham was *not justified by works;* St. James says he was *justified by works.* Do they not contradict each other?

A.--No: 1st, because they do not speak of the same justification. St. Paul speaks of that justification which was when Abraham was seventy-five years old, about twenty years before Isaac was born. St. James of that justification which was when he offered up Isaac on the altar.

2d. Because they do not speak of the same works : St. Paul speaking of works that precede faith; St. James, of works that spring from it.

Q. 15--In what sense is Adam's sin imputed to all mankind?

A.--In Adam all die, i. e., 1st, Our bodies there became mortal; 2d, Our souls dies, i. e., were disunited from God; and hence, 3d, We are all born with a sinful, devilish nature, by reason whereof: 4th, We are children of wrath, liable to death eternal.--Rom. v, 18; Eph. ii, 3.

Q. 16--In what sense is the righteousness of Christ imputed to all mankind, or to believers?

A.--We do not find it expressly affirmed in Scripture, that God imputes the righteousness of Christ to any. Although we do find, thath is imputed to us for righteousness.

That text, as by one man's disobedience all men were made sinners, so by the obedience of one, all were made righteous we conceive means by the merits of Christ, all men are cleared from the guilt of Adam's actual transgression.

We conceive further, That through the obedience and death of Christ, 1st, The bodies of all men became immortal after the resurrection; 2d, Their souls receive a capacity or spiritual life; and 3d. An actual spark or seed thereof; 4th,

All believers become children of grace, reconciled to God; and 5th, Made partakers of the divine nature.

Q. 17--Have we not, then, unawares, leaned too much towards *Calvanism?*

A.--We are afraid we have.

Q. 18--Have we not also leaned towards *Antinomianism?*

A.--We are afraid we have.

Q. 19--What is *Antinomiansim?*

A.--The doctrines which make void the law through faith.

Q. 20--What are the main pillars thereof?

A.--1st, That Christ abolished the moral law; 2d, That therefore Christians are not obliged to observe it. 3d, That one branch of Christian liberty, is liberty from obeying the commandments of God. 4th, That it is a bondage to do a thing because it is commanded, or forebear it because it is forbidden; 5th, That a believer is not obliged to use the ordinances of God to do good works; 6th, That a preacher ought not to exhort to good works, not unbelievers, because it is hurtful, nor believers, because it is needless.

Q. 21--What was the occasion of St. Paul's writing his epistle to the *Galatians?*

A.--The coming of certain men amongst the *Galatians,* who taught, Except ye be circumcised and keep the law of Moses, ye cannot be saved.

Q. 22--What is his main design herein?

A.--To prove, 1st, that no man can be saved, or justified by the works of the law, either moral or ritual; 2d, That every believer in *Christ* is justified by faith without the works of the law.

Q. 23--What does he mean by the works of the law? Gal. ii, 16; &c.

A.--All works which do not spring from faith in Christ.

Q. 24--What by being under the law? Gal. iii, 23.

A.--Under the Mosaic dispensation.

Q. 25--What law has Christ abolished?

A.--The ritual law of Moses.

Q. 26--What is meant by liberty? Gal. v, 1.

A.--Liberty, 1st from the law, 2d, from sin.

2d. Q. 1. How comes what is written on justification to be so intricate and obscure? Is this obscurity from the nature of the thing itself, or from the fault or weakness of those who generally treated about it?

A.--We apprehend this obscurity does not arise from the nature of the subject, but partly from the extreme warmth of most writers who have treated of it.

Q. 2. We affirm faith in *Christ* is the sole condition of justification. But does not repentance go before that faith?--Yea, and (supposing there be opportunity for them) fruits or works meet for repentance?

A.--Without doubt they do.

Q. 3. How then can we deny them to be conditions of justifications? Is not this a mere strife of words?

A.--It seems not, though it has been grievously abused. But so the abuse cease, let the use remain.

Q. 4. Shall we read over together Mr. Baxter's aphorsims concerning justification?

A.--By all means.

Q. 5. Is an assurance of God's pardoning love absolutely necessary to our being in his favor? Or may there possibly be some exempt cases?

A.--We dare not positively say there are not.

Q. 6. Is such an assurance absolutely necessary to inward and outward holiness?

A.--To inward we apprehend it is: to outward holiness we incline to think not.

Q. 7. Is it indispensably necessary to final salvation?

A.--Love hopeth all things. We know not how far any may fall under the case of invincible ignorance,

Q. 8. But what can we say of one of our own society who dies without it, as I. W. at London?

A.--It may possibly be an exempt case (if the fact was really so.) But we determine nothing; we leave his soul in the hands of Him that made it.

Q. 9. Does a man believe any longer than he sees a reconciled God?

A.--We conceive not. But we allow there may be infinite degrees in seeing God; even as many as there are between him that sees the sun, when it shines on his eyelids closed, and him who stands with his eyes wide open in the full blaze of his beams.

Q. 10. Does a man believe any longer than he loves God?

A.--In no wise. For neither circumcision or uncircumcision avails, without faith working by love.

Q. 11. Have we duly considered the case of Cornelius? Was he not in the favor of God, when his prayers and alms came up for a memorial before God, i. e. before he believed in Christ?

A.--It does seem that he was, in some degree. But we speak not of those who have heard the gospel.

Q. 12. But were those works of his splendid sins?

A.--No; nor were they done without the grace of Christ.

Q. 13. How then can we maintain, that all works done before we have a sense of the pardoning love of God, are sin? And, as such, an abomination to Him?

A.--The works of him who has heard the gospel, and does not believe, are not done as God hath willed or commanded them to be done. And yet we know not how to say that they are an abomination to the Lord in him who feareth God, and from that principle does the best he can.

Q. 14. Seeing there is so much difficulty in this subject, can we deal too tenderly with them that oppose us?

A.--We cannot, unless we were to give up any part of the truth of God.

Q. 15. Is a believer constrained to obey God?

A.--At first, he often is. The love of Christ constraineth him. After this he may obey, or he may not; no constraint being laid on him.

Q. 16. Can faith be lost but through disobedience?

A.--It cannot. A believer first inwardly disobeys, inclines to sin with his heart; then his intercourse with God is cut off, i. e. his faith is lost. And after this he may fall into outward sin, being now weak and like another man.

Q. 17. How can such a one recover faith?

A.--By repenting and doing the first works. Rev. ii c. 5 v.

Q. 18. Whence is it that so great a majority of those who believe, fall more or less into doubt or fear?

A.--Chiefly from their own ignorance or unfaithfulness; often from their not watching unto prayer, perhaps from some defect, or want of the power of God, in the preaching they hear.

Q. 19. Is there not a defect in us? Do we preach as we did at first? Have we not changed our doctrines?

A.--1st, At first we preached almost wholly to unbelievers. To those therefore we speak almost continually of remission of sins through the death of Christ, and the nature of faith in his blood. And so we do still among those who need to be taught the first elements of the gospel of Christ.

2d. But those in whom the foundation is already laid we exhort to go on to perfection which we did not see so clearly at first, although we occasionally spoke of it from the beginning.

3d. Yet we now preach, and that continually, faith in Christ, as our prophet, priest and king, at least as clearly, as strongly, and as fully, as we did several years ago.

Q. 20. Do not some of our preachers preach too much of the wrath, and too little of the love of God?

A.--We fear that they have leaned to that extreme, and hence some of their hearers have lost the joy of faith.

Q. 21. Need we ever preach the terrors of the Lord to those who know they are accepted of Him?

A.--No, it is folly so to do; for love is to them the strongest of all motives.

Q. 22. Do we ordinarily represent a justified state so great and happy as it is?

A.--Perhaps not; a believer walking in the light, is inexpressibly great and happy.

Q. 23. Should we not have a care of depreciating justification, in order to exalt the state of full sanctification?

A.--Undoubtedly we should beware of this; for one may insensibly slide into it.

Q. 24. How should we avoid it?

A.--When we are going to speak of entire sanctification, let us first describe the blessings of a justified state, as strong as possible.

Q. 25. Does not the truth of the gospel lie very near both to Calvanism and Antinomianism?

A.--Indeed it does, as it were within a hair's breadth. So that it is altogether foolish and sinful, because we do not altogether agree with one or the other, to run from them as far as ever we can.

Q. 26. Wherein may we come to the very verge of Calvanism?

A.--1st. In ascribing all good to the free grace of God. 2d. In denying all natural free will, and all power antecedent to grace; and 3d In excluding all merit from man; even for what he has or does for the grace of God.

Q. 27. Wherein may we come to the edge of Antinomianism?

A.--1st in exalting the merits and love of Christ. 2d. In rejoicing evermore.

Q. 28. Does faith supersede, (set aside the necessity of) holiness of good works?

A.--In no wise. So far from it that it implies both as a cause does its effects.

III. Q. 1. Can an unbeliever (whatever he be in other respects) challenge anything of God's justice?

A.--He cannot, nothing but hell. And this is a point which we cannot insist too much on.

Q. 2. Do we exempt men of their own righteousness, as we did at first? Do we sufficiently labor when they begin to be convinced of sin, to take away all they lean upon? Should we not then endeavor with all our might, to overturn their false foundations?

A.--This was at first one of our principal points. And it ought to be so still-- For, till all other foundations are overturned, they cannot build on Christ.

Q. 3. Did we not then purposely throw them into convictions. Into strong sorrow and fear. Nay, did we not strive to make them inconsolable? Refusing to be comforted?

A.--We did. And so should we do still, for the stronger the conviction, the speedier is the deliverance. And none so soon receive the peace of God, as those who steadily refuse all other comfort.

Q. 4. What is sincerity?

A.--Willingness to know and to do the whole will of God. The lowest species thereof seems to be faithfulness in that which is little.

Q. 5. Has God any regard for man's sincerity?

A.--So far, that no man in any state can possibly please God without it; neither in any moment wherein he is not sincere.

Q. 6. But can it be conceived that God has any regard to the sincerity of an unbeliever?

A.--Yes, so much, that if he perseveres therein, God will infallibly give him faith.

Q. 7. What regard may we conceive him to have to the sincerity of a believer?

A.--So much, that in every sincere believer he fulfils all the great and precious promises.

Q. 8. Whom do you term a sincere believer?

A.--One that walks in the light, as God is in the light.

Q. 9. Is sincerity the same with a single eye?

A.--Not altogether; the latter refers to our intentions; the former to our wills or desires.

Q. 10. Is it not all in all?

A.--All will follow persevering sincerity. God gives every thing with it; nothing without it.

Q. 11. Are not, then, sincerty and faith equivalent terms?

A.--By no means. Is it at least nearly related to works as it is to faith? For example; who is sincere before he believes? He that then does all he can; he that, according to the power he has received, brings forth fruit meet for repentance.-- Who is sincere after he believes? He that, from a sense of God's love, is zealous of all good works.

Q. 12. Is it no sincerity what St. Paul terms a willing mind? 2 Cor. viii, 12.

A.--Yes, if the word be taken in a general sense. For it is a constant disposition to use all the grace given.

Q. 13. But do we not then set sincerity on a level with faith?

A.--No; for we allow a man may be sincere and not be justified, as he may be penitent and not be justified: (not as yet) but he cannot have faith, and not be justified. The very moment he believes, he is justified.

Q. 14. But do we not give up faith and put sincerity in its place, as the condition of our acceptance with God?

A.--We believe it is one condition of our acceptance, as repentance likewise is. And we believe it a condition of our continuing in state of acceptance with God. Yet we do not put it in the place of faith. It is by faith the merits of Christ are applied to my soul. But if I am not sincere they are not applied.

Q. 15. Is not this that going about to establish your own righteousness, whereof Paul speaks?

A.--St. Paul there minifestly speaks of unbelievers who sought to be accepted for the sake of their own righteousness. We do not seek to be accepted for the sake of our sincerity; but through the merits of Christ alone. Indeed, so long as any man believes, he cannot go about (in St. Paul's sense,) to establish his own righteousness.

Q. 16. But do you consider that we are under the covenant of grace? And that the covenant of works is now abolished?

A.--All mankind are under the covenant of grace, from the very hour that the original promise was made. If by the covenant of works you mean that of unsinning obedience made with Adam before the fall; no man but Adam was ever under that covenant--for it was abolished before *Cain* was born. Yet it is not so abolished, but that will stand, in a measure, even to the end of the world, i. e. if we do this we shall live; if not we shall die eternally; if we do well we shall live with God in glory--if evil, we shall die the second death. For every man shall be judged in that, and rewarded according to his works.

Q. 17. What means then, to him that believeth, his faith is counted for righteousness?

A.--That God forgives him that is unrighteous as soon as he believes, accepting his faith instead of perfect righteousness. But then observe, universal righteousness follows, though it did not precede faith?

Q. 18. But is faith thus counted to us for righteousness, at whatsoever time we believe?

A.--Yes; in whatsoever moment we believe, all our past sins vanish away. They flee, as though they never had been, and we stand clear in the sight of God.

Q. 19. Are not the assurance of faith, the inspiration of the Holy Ghost, and the revelation of Christ in us, terms of nearly the same import?

A.--He that denies one of them, must deny all; they are so closely connected together.

Q. 20. Are they ordinarily, where the pure gospel is preached, essential to our acceptance?

A.--Undoubtedly they are, and as such to be insisted on, in the strongest terms.

Q. 21. Is not the whole dispute of salvation by faith, or by works, a mere strife of words?

A.--In asserting salvation by faith, we mean this: 1st, That pardon (salvation begun) is received by faith, producing works. 2d. That holiness, (salvation continued) is faith working by love. 3d. That Heaven (salvation finished) is the reward of this faith.

If you assert salvation by works, or by faith and works, mean the same thing, (understanding by faith, the revelation of Christ in us, by salvation, pardon, holiness, glory) we will not strive with you all. If you do not, this is not a strife of words, but the very vitals, the essence of Christianity is the thing in question.

Q. 22. Wherein does our doctrine now differ from that preached by Mr. Wesley at Oxford.

A.--Chiefly in these two points: 1st. He then knew nothing of that righteousness of faith in justification; nor 2d. Or that nature of faith itself, as implying consciousness of pardon.

Q. 23. May not some degree of the love of God go before a distinct sense of justification?

A.--We believe it may.

Q. 24. Can any degree of holiness or sanctification?

A.--Many degrees of outward holiness may; yea, and some degree of meekness, and several other tempers which would be branches of Christian holiness, but that they do not spring from christian principles. For the abiding love of God cannot spring but from faith in a pardoning God. And no true christian holiness can exist without that love of God for its foundation.

Q. 25. Is every man, as soon as he believes, a new creature, sanctified, pure in heart? Has he then a new heart? Does Christ dwell therein? and is he a temple of the Holy Ghost?

A.--All these things may be affirmed of every believer, in a true sense. Let us not, therefore, contradict those who maintain it. Why should we contend about words?

IV. Q. 1. How much is allowed by our brethren who differ from us with regard to sanctification?

A.--They grant 1st, That every one must be entirely sanctified in the article of death.

2d, That until then a believer daily grows in grace, comes nearer and nearer to perfection.

3d, That we ought to be continually pressing after this, and exhort all others so to do.

Q. 2. What do we allow them?

A.--We grant, 1st That many of those who have died in the faith, yea, the greater part of those we have known, were not sanctified throughout, not made perfect in love, till a little before death.

2d, That the term "sanctified["] is continually applied by St. Paul to all that were justified, were true believers.

3d, That by this term alone, he rarely (if ever) means saved from all sin.

4th, That, consequently, it is not proper to use it in this sense without adding the words "entirely, wholly," or the like.

5th, That the inspired writers almost continually speak of, or to those who were justified, but very rarely, either of or to those who were wholly sanctified.

6th, That, consequently, it behooves us to speak in public almost continually of the state of justification; but more rarely, at least, in full and explicit terms concerning entire sanctification.

Q. 3. What, then, is the point wherein we divide?

A --It is this: Whether we should expect to be saved from all sin, before the article of death.

Q. 4. Is there any clear Scripture *promise* of this? That God will save us from all sin?

A.--There is, Psalm cxxx. 8: "He shall redeem Israel from all his sins."

This is more largely expressed in the prophecy of Ezekiel. "Then will I sprinkle clean water upon you and you shall be clean from all your filthiness, and from all your idols will I cleanse you--I will also save you from all your uncleanliness" cxxxvi, 25, 29. No promise can be more clear. And to this the Apostle plainly refers in that exhortation. Having these promises, let us cleanse ourselves from all filthiness of the flesh and spirit, perfecting holiness in the fear of God. 2 Cor. vii, 1. Equally clear and expressive is that ancient promise: The Lord thy God will circumcise thy heart, and the heart of thy seed, to love the Lord thy God with all thy heart, and with all thy soul. Deut. xxx. 6.

Q. 5. But does any assertion answerable to this occur in the New Testament?

A --There does, and that laid down in the plainest terms. See 1 John iii, 8: For this purpose the Son of God was manifested, that he might destroy the works of the Devil. The works of the Devil, without any limitation or restriction; but all sin is the work of the Devil. Parallel to which is that assertion of St. Paul, Eph, v. 27, Christ loved the Church, and gave himself for it, that he might present it to himself a glorious church, not having spot or wrinkle, or any such thing, but that it should be holy, and without blemish.

And to the same effect is that assertion in the 8th chapter of the Romans, (3d and 4th verses God sent his Son, that the righteousness of the law might be fulfilled in us, walking not after the flesh, but after the spirit.

Q. 6. Does the New Testament afford any further ground for expecting to be saved from all sin?

A.--Undoubtedly it does, both in those prayers and commands which are equivalent to the strongest assertions.

Q. 7. What prayers do you mean?

A.--Prayers for entire sanctification; which, were there no such thing, would be mere mockery of God. Such in particular, are 1st, Deliver us from evil; or rather from the evil one. Now, when this is done, when we are delivered from all evil, there can be no sin remaining.

2d. Neither pray I for these alone, but for them also which shall believe on me through their word, that they may be all one, as thou, Father art in me, and I in thee, that they also may be one of us; I in them, and thou in me, that they may be made perfect in one. John c, xvii, v. 20, 21, 23.

3. I bow my knees unto the God and Father of our Lord Jesus Christ, that he would grant you, that ye being rooted and grounded in love, may be able to comprehend with all saints, what is the length, breadth and heighth, and to know the love of Christ, which passeth knowledge, that ye might be filled with the fullness of God. Eph. c. iii, v. 14, 16, 19.

4. The very God of peace sanctify you wholly. And I pray God; your whole spirit, soul, and body be preserved blameless unto the coming of our Lord Jesus Christ, 1 Thess. v. 23.

Q. 8. What command is there to the same effect?

A.--1. Be ye perfect as your Father which is in heaven is perfect. Math. c. v. 48 v.

2. Thou shalt love the Lord thy God with all thy heart, and with all thy soul, and with all thy mind. Math. c. xxii. v. 37. But if the love of God fill all the heart, there can be no sin there.

Q. 9. But how does it appear that this is to be done before the article of death.

A.--First, from the very nature of a command, which is not given to the dead, but to the living.

Therefore, Thou shalt love the Lord thy God with all thy heart, cannot mean, Thou shalt do this when thou diest, but while thou livest.

Secondly, from express texts of Scripture.

1. The grace of God which bringeth salvation hath appeared to all men teaching us, that having renounced ungodliness and worldly lusts, we should live righteously, soberly and godly, in the present world; looking for the glorious appearing of our Lord Jesus Christ, who gave himself for us, that he might redeem us from all iniquity, and purify unto himself a peculiar people, zealous of good works. Tit. ii, v. 11, 14.

2. He hath raised up an horn of salvation for us, to perform the mercy promised to our fathers; the oath which he swore to our Father Abraham that he would grant unto us, that we being delivered out of the hands of all our enemies, should serve him without fear, in holiness and righteousness before him all the days of our life. Luke c. i. v. 69, &c.

Q. 10. Does not the harshly preaching perfection tend to bring believers into a kind of bondage or slavish fear?

A.--It does. Therefore, we should always place it in the most amiable light, so that it may excite only hope, joy and desire.

Q. 11. Why may we not continue in the joy of faith, even till we are made perfect?

A.--Why, indeed! Since holy grief does not quench this joy; since even while we are under the cross, while we deeply partake of the sufferings of Christ we may rejoice in with joy unspeakable.

Q. 12. Do we not discourage believers from rejoicing evermore.

A.--We ought not to do so. Let them all their time rejoice unto God, so it be with reverence. And even if lightness or pride should mix with their joy, let us not strike at the joy itself, (this is the gift of God,) but at that lightness or pride, that the evil may cease and the good remain.

Q. 13. Ought we to be anxiously careful about perfection, lest we should die before we have attained it?

A.--In no wise. We ought to be thus careful for nothing, neither spiritual nor temporal.

Q. 14. But ought we not to be troubled on account of the sinful nature which still remains in us?

A.--It is good to have a deep sense of this, and to be ashamed before the Lord. But this should only incite us the more earnestly to turn unto Christ every moment, and to draw light, and life, and strength from Him, that we may go on conquering and to conquer. And therefore, when the sense of our sin most abounds, the sense of his love should much more abound.

Q. 15. Will our joy or our trouble increase as we grow in grace?

A.--Perhaps both. But, without doubt. our joy in the Lord will increase as our love increases.

Q. 16. Is not the teaching believers to be continually pouring over their inbred sin, the ready way to make them forget that they were purged from their former sin?

A.--We find by experience it is; or to make them undervalue, and account it a little thing: whereas, indeed, (though there are still greater gifts behind,) this is inexpressible great and glorious.

DISCIPLINE.

ARTICLE I.
TITLE.

This connection shall be denominated "The African Union First Colored Methodist Protestant Church, in the United States of America and elsewhere," who may adopt our order and Book of Discipline.

ARTICLE II.
TERMS OF MEMBERSHIP.

1. There is only one condition required of those who apply for membership in an African Union First Colored Methodist Protestant Church, viz: A desire to flee from the wrath to come, and be saved by Grace through faith in our Lord Jesus Christ, with an avowed determination to walk in all the commandments of God, blameless. But those who may continue therein must give evidence of their desire and determination, by conforming to such moral discipline as the word of God requires.

2. There shall be probationary privileges, in which persons shall be held as candidates for admission into membership in this Church, preparatory to their being received into full membership by a compliance with the terms thereof.

3. The children of our members, and those under their guardianship, shall be recognized as enjoying probationary privileges, and held as candidates for membership, and may be put into classes, as such, with the consent of their parents or guardians. But such membership shall not be recognized as enjoying such privileges unless the children are under serious consideration concerning their souls, and after six months probation they may be admitted members with the consent of the Church.

ARTICLE III.
DIVISION INTO DISTRICTS, CIRCUITS AND STATIONS.

1. Those parts of the United States embraced by the African Union First Colored Methodist Protestant Church, shall be divided into districts, and the following shall be the Districts.--New York, Rhode Island and all the Eastern

States be the Eastern District; Delaware, New Jersey and Pennsylvania be the Middle District; and all the Southern States be the Southern District, the same having their respective boundaries. The Middle District cedes to the Eastern District the north-eastern part of Pennsylvania and New Jersey, commencing at Jersey City, running a north-westerly line to Susquehanna city, from thence along the Warren county line, subject to those alterations which may be made or authorized from time to time by the General Conference.

2. Each District shall be divided into Circuits and Stations, by its Annual Conference.

3. Every Minister or Preacher, removing from one District to another, and every member removing from one circuit, station, or church, to another, having a certificate of his or her good standing, shall be entitled to membership in any other district, circuit or station of the African Union First Colored Methodist Protestant Church, within the limits of this Church to which he or she may apply for membership.

ARTICLE IV.
ON RECEIVING CHURCHES, &c.

1. Any number of beleivers united into a religious Society or Church, embracing the principles of religious truth held by this Discipline, adopting this connection and conforming to our Book of Discipline and means of Grace, shall, at their request made to the President of the District or Annual Conference, or to the Minister of a circuit or station, be recognized as an African Union First Colored Methodist Protestant Church, and be entitled to all the privileges granted by this Discipline, subject, however, to the decision of the most adjacent quarterly conference.

2. Every church or society shall be composed of any number of members residing sufficiently near each other to assemble statedly for public worship, and to transact its temporal business; and every church shall be divided, when it becomes necessary, into smaller companies or classes, for the purpose of religious instruction or edification.

3. Every church or society shall have power, by the concurrence of a majority of two-thirds of its qualified members present, at any called meeting for the purpose, to purchase, build, lease, sell, rent, or otherwise obtain or dispose of

property, for the mutual benefit of the Church[.] Each Church shall also have power to admit persons into full membership, and to try, censure or expel, unworthy members, in accordance with the provision of this Discipline, and the rules thereof.

4. But no Church whatever shall be in connection with this Church, which does not conform to this Book of Discipline, and the regulations thereof, or which may hereafter reject any part or provision thereof.

ARTICLE V.
LEADERS MEETING.

1. Once a week in every station, and once a month in every circuit, there shall be a leaders meeting, composed of all the Preachers, Exhorters, Class Leaders, Stewards and Trustees, to receive what monies they have collected for the Preachers Poor or Church, and report all members that are sick, and any one that walks disorderly, and will not be reproved, and make appointments to preach. The Minister in charge shall be the chairman of the meeting, or appoint some one in his place.

2. The duty of Preachers and Exhorters is to attend the leaders meeting, and there receive their appointment. If he fails to fill the appointment, the Preacher or Exhorter so failing, and neglecting to render a satisfactory excuse to the official board, for such neglect, the Minister or Exhorter so offending shall be silenced for three months for the first offence; for the second six months; and for the third offence, one year.

ARTICLE VI.
QUARTERLY CONFERENCES.

1. There shall be four Quarterly Conferences in each circuit and station, in every Conference year, to be composed of all the Ministers, Preachers, Exhorters, Trustees, Stewards and Class Leaders, in full membership, belonging to the Circuit or station, provided that the Minister shall have authority to call special meetings of the Quarterly Conference at other times, when circumstances make it necessary.

2. Each Quarterly Conference shall be vested with power to examine into the official character of all its members, and to admonish or reprove, as occasion

may require[.] To grant to persons properly qualified and recommended by the class of which the applicant is a member, license to preach and exhort, and renew their license annually. To admit Ministers from religious denominations to membership, who may come properly recommended, and receive all Ministers and Preachers, coming from our associated Churches with valid certificate. To recommend Ministers and Preachers to the Annual Conference; to travel, and for ordination; to hear or decide on appeals and to perform such other duties as are authorized by the General Conference, *Provided,* nevertheless, that no person shall be licensed to preach until he or they have shall been first examined and recommended by a committee of five, composed of Minister and Laymen chosen by the Quarterly Conference.

The Order of Business:--1. The examination of members official characters. 2. Are there any applications for license to preach or exhort? 3. Are there any licenses to be renewed? 4. Are there any applications to join this Conference, and how long have they been connected with this Church and Connection? 5. Are there any Ministers or Preachers to be recommended to the Annual Conference? 6. Are there any appeals? 7. How many members in society? 8. How many have been received by certificate? 9. How many have been expelled? 10. How many removed without certificate? 11. How many removed by certificate? 12. What is the increase this quarter? 13. How many on probation? 14. How many laid aside for breach of our rules? 15. How many members have died this quarter? 16. Who are they? 17. How many in sabbath schools? 18. What have the Ministers received this quarter? 19. What has been collected for the President this quarter? 20. What has been collected for the Sabbath schools this quarter? 21. What has been collected for the missionaries and worn out preachers cause this quarter?

Questions of examination to be asked candidates for licenses:

The following questions shall be asked of each candidate, and if he or they answer them satisfactorily, he or they may be licensed:

Q. 1. Have you faith in Christ, and are you striving to be holy in heart and all manner of conversation?

Q. 2. Have you any other motive in requesting license to preach than a desire to be instrumental in edifying the Church of God, calling sinners to repentance, and saving your soul, and those who hear you?

Q. 3. Do you believe that the Holy Scriptures of the Old and New Testament contain all things necessary to salvation?

Q. 4. Have you examined our Constitution and Book of Discipline?

Q. 5. Do you approve of them?

Q. 6. Are you willing to comply with their requirements?

Q. 7. Are you solvent?

Questions to be answered by the members of the Quarterly Conferences:--

1. Have they gifts as well as graces for the work? 2. Have they in some tolerable degree a clear, sound understanding, a right judgement in the things of God, a just conception of salvation by faith, and has God given them any degee of utterance? 3. Do they speak readily, clearly and justly? 4. Have they fruits? 5. Are any truly convinced of sin and converted to God by their labors? As long as these remarks concur in any one, we believe him or they are called of God to preach, and may be licensed.

ARTICLE VII.
COMPOSITION AND POWERS OF THE ANNUAL CONFERENCE.

1. There shall be held annually within the limits of each District, a Conference, to be denominated the Annual Conference, composed of all the ordained ministers and local preachers belonging to the District; that is, all ministers properly under the stationing authority of the Conference, and stewards of this Conference. Each Conference shall regulate the manner of elections in its own District; *Provided,* However, that the election to the first Annual Conference, under this Discipline, shall be according to such regulations as may be adopted by the Quarterly Conferences of the respective circuits and stations. Each circuit or station is entitled to one lay delegate to the Annual Conference of its District.

2. The Annual Conferences shall be vested with power to elect a President annually, to raise a fund for the support of the superannuated and worn out

preachers and missionaries, and a general fund for the support of the Conference, and a home and foreign mission fund.

3. And to examine into the official conduct of all its members, to receive by vote, such ministers and preachers into the Conference, as come properly recommended, and who can be efficiently employed as itinerant preachers or missionaries; to elect to order those who are eligible and competent to the pastoral office; to hear and decide on appeal; to define and regulate the boundaries of circuits and stations; to station the ministers, preachers, and missionaries, and to perform such other duties as are prescribed by this Conference, or may be prescribed by the General Conferences.

4. Each circuit or station is entitled to one delegate to the Annual Conference of its district.

The Annual Conference respectively shall also have authority to perform the following additional duties:

1st. To make such rules and regulations as the peculiarities of the District may require; *Provided,* However, that no rule or regulation be made inconsistent with this Discipline; and *Provided,* furthermore, that the General Conference shall have power to annual any rule or regulation which that body may deem undisciplined.

2nd. To prescribe and regulate the mode of stationing the ministers and preachers within the District; *Provided,* always, that they grant each minister or preacher stationed, an appeal during the sitting of Conference.

3rd. Each Annual Conference shall have exclusive power to make its own rules and regulations for admission and government of its members within its District. But neither the General nor any Annual Conference shall assume powers to interfere with the constitutional powers of the civil governments or with the operation of civil laws; yet nothing herein contained shall be so construed as to authorize or sanction anything inconsistent with the morality of the holy scriptures.

4th. Each Annual Conference shall keep a journal of its proceedings, and send a copy to the General Conference, and shall make such rules and regulations as may be necessary for its publication.

WHEREAS, We, the General Conference, now in session, see the great necessity of sustaining our ministers,

Resolved, That we do hereby recommend to all our churches the propriety of giving their ministers a liberal support and that they use every means in their power to accomplish the same. Therefore it shall be the duty of each church or circuit, or station, that receives a minister sent to them from the Conference to make their agreement according to their constitution and the Godly judgment of its laity; for the support of the same.

ORDER OF BUSINESS.

1. To hear the reports of all its members.

2. The examination of the official conduct and characters of its members.

3. The election of the President.

ANNUAL CONFERENCE QUESTIONS.

Question 1. How many societies have been organized this year?

Q. 2. How many have withdrawn from the Connection this year?

Q. 3. Are there any applications to join the Itinerancy or Conference?

Q. 4. Are there any applications for Deacon's orders.

Q. 5. Are there any applications for Elder's orders?

Q. 6. How many members in Church society?

Q. 7. How many Sabbath Schools, and number of scholars in each?

Q. 8. What have the ministers received this year?

Q. 9. What have the missionaries received this year?

Q. 10. What has the President received this year?

Q. 11. What has been collected for defraying the expenses of the Conference?

Q. 12. What has been collected for the support of the missionary cause this year?

Q 13. Are the candidates qualified for the itinerancy?

Q. 14. Have all the ministers enforced the book of Discipline within the station and circuit of their charge?

Q. 15. Have all the ministers sustained their characters?

Q. 16. Who has been expelled this year?

Q. 17. Are there any appeals this year?

Q. 18. Who has located this year?

Q. 19. Are there any applications for ministers?

Q. 20. Who has died this year?

Q. 21. Are any supernumery?

Q. 22. Are there any superannuated?

Q. 23. Who has withdrawn this year?

Q. 24. Where are the ministers stationed this year?

Q. 25. Where shall our next Annual Conference meet?

THE GENERAL CONFERENCE MEMBERS.

Question 1. Who are the members of the General Conference?

Answer. All Ministers who have been duly elected by the Annual Conference; *Provided* the Annual Conference do not elect any Ministers that have not traveled two years previous to the sitting of the Annual Conference so electing.

ARTICLE VIII.
COMPOSITION OF THE GENERAL CONFERENCES.

1. There shall be a General Conference of this Connection every four years, on the last Saturday in August, in such place as may be determined on by the Conference.

2. The General Conference shall consist of an equal number of Ministers and laymen. The ratio of representation of each District shall be one Minister and one layman for every hundred persons in full membership; *Provided,* however, that any District which may not have one hundred members, shall be entitled to two representatives, one Minister and one layman, until a different ratio shall be fixed by the General Conference.

3. The General Conference shall elect a President to preside over its deliberations, and one or more Secretaries to serve during the sitting of Conference; it shall also judge election returns and qualifications of its members, and form its own rules of order. A majority of all the Representatives shall constitute a quorum.

4. The Ministers and laymen shall deliberate in one body; but if upon the final passage of any question it be required by three members, the Ministers and laymen of both classes of Representatives shall be necessary to constitute a vote of the Conference. A similar regulation shall be observed by the Annual Conference.

5. The yeas and nays shall be recorded at the call of the majority of the members present.

ARTICLE IX.
POWERS OF THE GENERAL CONFERENCE.

1. The General Conference shall have power to make rules and regulations for the Itinerant Ministers, Missionary, Literary, and every other department of the Church recognized by this Discipline.

2. To define and regulate the boundaries of the respective Annual Conference Districts; *Provided,* however, that the Annual Conferences of any two or more Districts shall have power, by mutual agreement, to alter their respective adjoining boundaries, or to unite and become one District, or to set off a new District, to receive into their respective limits and jurisdiction any station or circuit which does not belong to some other District; but every alteration made in the boundaries of the respective Districts shall be reported to the ensuing General Conference.

3. The General Conference shall publish such parts of the journal of its proceedings as it may deem requisite.

4. All papers, books, &c., belonging to the Conference shall be preserved as that body may direct.

ARTICLE X.
DUTY OF THE PRESIDENT OF THE DISTRICT.

1. The duty of the President shall be, in the absence of the Annual Conference, to hold himself in readiness, when called on, to organize Churches and to receive said Churches into the Connection as candidates to the Annual Conference

2. The President, if any difficulty arises in the District among the churches, circuits or stations, shall call two or more of the Elders of his District, and for the want of Elders, Traveling Deacons, and for want of Deacons, Traveling Preachers, and form a Conference, and settle and arrange the matter until the ensuing Annual Conference.

3. The President shall receive all charges or complaints against Ministers or Traveling Preachers until the sitting of the Annual Conference, and to visit

through his District at least twice a year, and make his report to the Annual Conference.

ARTICLE XI.
DUTIES OF THE MINISTER IN CHARGE.

1. The duty of the Minister in charge shall be, to be faithful in the discharge of his duties in preaching, holding his quarterly meetings, love feasts, administering the Lord's supper, visiting the sick, burying the dead, and baptizing and taking care of his flock in trust; to be punctual in attending his Annual and General Conferences and sustaining the Discipline, and to read a portion of it to his congregation once every quarter.

2. The Minister shall not be tedious in preaching, nor suffer the practice by any Minister or Preacher in his charge. He shall also establish Sabbath Schools in his charge where there is none, and try to raise literary societies for the improvement of his people.

VISITATION OF THE SICK.

If the Minister find the person to be grossly ignorant, he shall instruct him or her in the nature of repentance and faith, and in the way of acceptance with God through the Mediator and atonement of Jesus Christ.

If the sick person appear to be a stupid, thoughtless and hardened sinner, the Minister shall endeavor to awaken his mind, to arouse his conscience, to convince him of the evil and danger of sin, and of the curse of the law and the wrath of God due the sinners; to bring him to an humble and penitential sense of his iniquities, and then to state before him the fullness of the grace and mercy of God in and through the merits of the Redeemer; the absolute necessity of faith and repentance, in order to his being interested in the favor of God, and his obtaining everlasting happiness.

If the sick person appear to be broken in spirit, with a sense of sin and apprehensions of the Divine displeasure, let consolation be administered, encouragement, setting before him the free richness of the grace of God, and the precious promises of the Gospel made to all penitents.

In a word, it is the duty of Ministers and pious persons, when visiting the sick, to pray with and for them, and to administer instruction, conviction, support, consolation or encouragement, as the case may seem to require; and to improve the occasion to exhort those about them, to consider their morality, and turn to the Lord, and make peace with Him, and in health prepare for sickness, death, and judgment.

ARTICLE XII.
DUTIES OF THE CLASS LEADERS.

1. It shall be the duty of the class leader to meet his class once a week, to inquire into the state of and condition of each member; to exhort, reprove, admonish or encourage, as the case may require, to receive from each member what they are willing to give for the Church, Minister or poor; report his class once every Quarterly Conference.

2. If any members absent themselves from class for three successive weeks, the leader of such members shall visit and kindly admonish them, and if they do not amend he shall give their names to the Minister in charge for neglect of duty, who shall deal with such members according to the Discipline.

3. The leader shall give no love feast tickets to members who absent themselves from their classes for three successive weeks, without a lawful excuse, nor shall they be admitted thereto.

ARTICLE XIII.
DUTY OF MEMBERS.

1. To attend public worship, public and family prayer; to meet their class once a week, at the place and time appointed; to be present at the time of the administration of the Lord's Supper, and to partake of the same.

2. And it shall be the duty of each member to be faithful in paying their tithes for the support of the Church and Ministry, and to do all in their power to help support their Minister

3. All worthy members of our Church, wishing to withdraw from us, shall make it known to the Minister in charge, who shall give them a certificate of their good standing.

ARTICLE XIV.
STIPENDARY FUND.

1. The Minister of each circuit or station shall provide a stipendary fund, to compensate the President of his District for his services; and to instruct his people to collect monies for such fund.

2. It shall be the duty of each member of the Connection to pay a stipulated sum of three cents per month, as a sinking fund, to be applied to bear the expenses of the spiritual concerns of the church, and Connection, and shall be collected by the class leaders, and paid to the Steward, and shall be paid out by order of the official board, taking his receipt for the same

3. The President shall receive from the Steward, his salary, out of this fund. The Steward shall make his report to the Annual Conference, each conference year; and for neglect of duty shall be brought to trial before the Quarterly Conference.

4. There shall be one or more Stewards in each circuit or station, whose duty it shall be to keep a general financial record between the official Ministers and President, and report quarterly and annually thereof.

ARTICLE XV.
APPLICATIONS FOR MINISTERS.

1. All Churches shall have the privilege of electing their Minister, previous to the sitting of the Annual Conference, and sending their petition to the Annual Conference for such Minister, and the Annual Conference shall appoint such Minister, said Minister accepting the appointment.

2. No Minister shall remain on a circuit or station over two years, but in case of necessity he may remain three years, but no longer.

ARTICLE XVI.
CHURCH PROPERTY.

The Discipline of the African Union First Colored Methodist Protestant Church shall not interfere with the constitutional rights of any of the Churches in any one State; its parsonage, money, property, school houses, &c.

ARTICLE XVII.
TRIAL OF EXHORTERS, CLASS LEADERS, TRUSTEES, STEWARDS AND MEMBERS.

If any member violate the rules of our Discipline, the person so offending shall visit him alone, and if the person so offending hear him, he has gained his brother, and the matter is at an end; but if the member offending will not hear him, he shall then inform the leader of the offending person, whose duty it shall be to see the offended and the offending members face to face, before witnesses, and if the member still refuse to hear or retract, it shall then be the duty of the leader of the member or members to present the case to the Minister in charge, who shall summon the member or members before the Church for trial, whose action shall be final; nevertheless, any member so expelled may have an appeal to the ensuing Quarterly Conference, on giving notice at the trial, and all appeals shall be final.

1. Question. How shall accused persons be brought to trial?

Answer. Before a select committee of the society of which they are a member.

2. It shall consist of three, five or seven outside of the official board, if possible, in the following manner: Let the accused and the accuser be brought face to face, but if this cannot be done, let the next best evidence be procured.

3. If the person be found guilty, by a decision of a majority of the members, before whom she or he is brought to trial, and the crime be such as is expressly forbidden in the word of God, sufficient to exclude a person from the kingdom of grace and glory, the Minister in charge shall expel him or her.

4. If the accused person evade a trial, by absenting himself, after sufficient notice be given him or them, and the circumstances of the case be strong and presumptive, let them be esteemed as guilty, and expelled.

5. Any member so expelled may have an appeal to the ensuing Quarterly Conference, on giving notice at the trial.

6. That in the selection of a committee of three--one by the minister, one by accused, one by the accuser. And in selection of five, one by the minister, one by

the accuser, one by the accused, and these three are to select the other two. In the choice of seven, two by the minister, one by the accused, one by the accuser, and these four to select the other three.

ARTICLE XVIII.
TRIAL OF LOCAL PREACHERS.

Any Local Preacher who violates our rules, laid down in our Discipline, and a charge be presented to the Minister in charge, he shall summon a committee of three Preachers, or for want of Preachers, exhorters or leaders, and call such accused person before the committee for investigation, and if he be found guilt he shall be silenced from officiating in public until the next Quarterly Conference, who shall try the case, and whose action shall be final; nevertheless such person may have an appeal to the next ensuing Annual Conference, by giving notice at the time to the Quarterly Conference. At the time set for trial, should the person absent himself from the Quarterly Conference, the trial shall proceed and witnesses be examined as though he was present.

ARTICLE XIX.
TRIAL OF TRAVELLING ELDERS, DEACONS OR PREACHERS.

If any of the travelling Elders, Deacons or Preachers, should be accused of any crime, a charge shall be made known to the class leader of the circuit or station, who shall speedily lay such charge before the official board, and they shall authorize one of them, if deemed necessary, to notify the President of the District, who, with the assistance of the next neighboring Elder, if there be no travelling Elder on the circuit or station, shall call him to an account and shall bring him to trial before a committee of travelling Preachers, or for want of travelling Preachers, local Elders, Decons, Preachers or Class Leaders; the committee to consist of not less than three[.] If possible, the accused and the accuser shall be brought face to face.

If the person be clearly convicted, he shall be suspended from all official standing in the Church until the ensuing Annual Conference, at which time his case shall be fully considered and determined.

If the accused and the accuser cannot be brought face to face, but the supposed delinquent flees from trial, it shall be received as a presumptive proof of guilt, "and out of the mouth of two or three witnesses" he shall be condemned--Nevertheless, even in that case, the Annual Conference shall reconsider and determine the whole matter.

ARTICLE XX.
TRIAL OF THE PRESIDENT.

During the interval of the Annual Conference, if the President should be accused of any crime, such as improper or gross conduct, or maladministration of law, or any crime that is forbidden in the word of God, let a charge be presented to to the official board, where such misdemeanor took place, the same shall notify the President of the adjoining District, forthwith of the nature of the crime, whose duty it shall be to call a committee of five travelling Elders, and for the want of Elders travelling Deacons, and for the want of Deacons travelling Preachers, and form a Conference, having previously notified the accused President of the time and place of trial, within his District, and try the case.

And should the accused be convicted, the same shall be suspended until the next Annual Conference. And the said Conference shall reconsider the case, and their decision shall be final.

If in the first case the President should be suspended, the committee shall have power to appoint a President until the ensuing Annual Conference.

PUBLIC WORSHIP.

The morning services on the Lord's day shall consist of singing a hymn, prayer, and reading a portion of the word of God, and an explanation thereon, then another hymn or a part of a hymn shall be sung, and an appropriate prayer addressed to the throne of grace, and the congregation dismissed.

The afternoon and evening services shall consist of the same exercises, except reading a portion of the Scripture, which may be omitted.

We recommend that no sermon exceed one hour, and that the Minister be not too tedious in conducting the other parts of divine worship.

It is further recommended that the Lord's Supper be repeated at the close of the first morning prayer.

During Public Worship the congregation is expected to attend with becoming gravity, abstaining from all salutation of persons present, or coming in ; and from gazing about, sleeping, smiling, whispering and all other unbecoming behaviour. The congregation are to avoid the common practice of standing about the Church door, before service, and of leaving the house before they are regularly dismissed.

Whilst the Minister is addressing the throne of Grace, the whole congregation should meekly kneel before God, and during the singing of the first hymn stand up with their faces towards the Minister, and assist in this delightful part of divine worship; the verses of the second hymn should be read over by the Minister, and sung by the people while seated.

We further recommend that all our members take their hymn books to Church with them, and sing with the spirit and with the understanding also. In administering the ordinance of burying the dead, let the form of Discipline be used.

MEANS OF GRACE.

The means of grace recognized by this Church are the public worship of Almighty God; searching the Scriptures; the Lord's Supper; Love Feasts; Class Meeting; Private and Family Prayer.

1. THE STUDY OF THE HOLY SCRIPTURES

Here but a few words are sufficient. No man, unless he knows and understands his duty, can discharge it as a virtue and with acceptance to God. This position is clear and incontrovertible. Our Saviour has stated it in a plain and emphatic declaration. "If ye know these things, happy are ye if ye do them." So far then, as duty is concerned, we acknowledge on all hands that the Bible is the great and sufficient source of light and instruction to us on every point of faith and practice. But this sacred book we should read and study, not only to make us wise in the sciences of salvation, to furnish us with the reasons and evidence of our faith, and with arguments to refute and repel the cavil of gainsayers, but also to sustain and console us with its rich and abundant promises on every occasion of mental depression and conflict. Says the Psalmist: "Thy word is a lamp unto my feet and a light unto my path; unless thy law had been my delight I should have perished in mine affliction." Such is the testimony of an ancient servant of God; a testimony which has been graciously repeated and realized a thousand times in every age of the Church. Let us all, therefore, make it a point of duty to read the word of God daily, and implore the divine blessing on our meditation, that His word may do us good, as it doth the upright in heart.

2. THE WORSHIP OF GOD.--PRIVATE PRAYER.

It is recommended, from the experience of pious and good men in all ages, as well as from the Holy Scriptures, that the people of God have daily their hours and seasons for mental retirement and devotion. This is a duty, which, in view of its absolute necessity to the inward discipline and comfort of the soul, and its many other advantages, ought always to be punctually attended to, and never neglected, and which should, in a manner, be estimated as the special medium of personal intercourse and communion with God. No one, indeed, can justly value the benefits of private prayer, but every one who has ever been regularly and habitually engaged in this duty, knows well to his pain and condemnation, how soon, upon the desertion of his closet, his soul has declined in the love and enjoyments of religion. Let every one of our members, then, be found statedly and punctually, three or four times in the day, upon his knees before God, and it will evidently appear how God rewards His people openly, and honors with His favors and blessings those who honor Him.

3. FAMILY WORSHIP.

This is all important to the purposes of family religion, and good domestic order and government. The effects produced thereby upon the minds of the children and domestics, and the comfort imparted by the same means to the heads of families themselves, are really incalculable. The voice of rejoicing and salvation is in the tabernacles of the righteous. Is this the testimony of eternal truth ? Let it not then be said of us, beloved brethren, that there is one household throughout our community in which the parents, and children, and servants are not regularly presented before God morning and evening in offices of prayer and praise. On this subject let none plead the want of talent or experience. It is the offering of the heart which God appreciates and accepts, and no doubt the special blessing of Heaven will descend upon that family wherein a portion of the Scriptures only are read as an act of sincere homage and devotion to the Almighty.

4. THE HOUSE OF GOD.

That kind of influence which family religion, regularly maintained, exerts over the domestic circle, the public worship of God, duly and statedly celebrated, extends over the community at large. Agreeably to the very spirit and nature of a religious profession, as well as the express letter of the New Testament, it must certainly be admitted that every member of the church is held responsible to attend the services of the house of God. "Forsake not the assembling of yourselves together," is a positive and sacred command. "Where even two or three are met together in my name, there am I in the midst of them," is a promise equally delightful and encouraging. As we then regard the authority of Jesus Christ, as we value the means which God himself has instituted and blessed a thousand times over; as we feel solicitous for the influence of Christianity upon public morals, as we are deeply concerned for the conversion of our children and our friends, as we are greatly interested for the revival and spread of the work of grace under our ministry, and the extending prosperity of our beloved Zion, as we hold all these objects dear to our hearts, let every African Union Colored Methodist Protestant be always ready to enter in at the sanctuary of Jehovah, and be seen in his proper place on the Lord's day.

In this connection we may make a remark upon the duty of punctual and devout attendance on those more intimate and social fellowships, known among us by the name of Class Meetings. The importance and advantages of this means of grace are not left to await the report of experiment. The edification and comfort derivable from them, their peculiar adaptation to unfold and improve the varieties and vicissitudes of religious experience, their precise accommodation to all the diversified shades of Christian trial and Christian character, can only be duly estimated by such as have mingled in those interesting and heavenly scenes, on occasions where the disconsolate have been relieved and blessed; the broken hearted penitent has found the Saviour of sinful men; the weak and the tempted have been strengthened and delivered; the doubting confirmed, and the faithful people of God have taken sweet counsel together, and felt their cup of spiritual joy to be full and overflowing.

If in any respect, Christian brethren, these meetings have degenerated under our notice and observation, it remains for us to endeavor, with the blessing of God, to revive them according to the genuine spirit of their original intention and tested excellence, and thus secure to our fellowship the benefits of an institution which God has so signally blessed, to thousands both in Europe and America.

ORDER FOR THE ADMINISTRATION OF THE LORD'S SUPPER.

On the day appointed for the celebration of the Lord's Supper, an appropriate discourse shall be delivered, after which a collection shall be taken for the relief of the poor. While the collectors are making the collection let the Minister repeat one or more of the following passages:

Let your light so shine before men that they may see your good works and glorify your Father which is in Heaven.--Matt. v-16.

Whatsoever ye would that men should do unto you, even so do unto them; for this is the law and the prophets.--Matt. vii-12

Not every one that saith unto me: Lord, Lord, shall enter into the Kingdom; but he that doeth the will of my Father who is in Heaven.--Matt. vii-21.

Zaccheus stood forth and said unto the Lord: Behold, the half of my goods I give to the poor, and if I have done any wrong to any man I restore him him fourfold.--Luke xix-8.

Godliness with contentment is great gain, for we brought nothing into this world and it is certain we can carry nothing out.--Tim. vi-6, 7.

To do good and to distribute, forget not; for with such sacrifices God is well pleased.--Heb. viii-16.

He that hath pity on the poor lendeth unto the Lord; and look what he layeth out, it shall be paid to him again.--Prov. xix.-17.

God is not unrighteous that he will forget your works and labors of love; which love ye have shewed for his name's sake, who have ministered unto the saints, and yet do minister.--Heb, vi.-10.

While these sentences are reading, some fit person, appointed, shall receive the alms for the poor in a decent basin, to be provided for that purpose; and then bring it to the Elder, who shall place it upon the table.

After which the Elder shall say:

Ye that do truly and earnestly repent of sin, and are in love and charity with your neighbors, and intend to lead a new life, following the commandments of God and walking from henceforth in his holy ways, draw near with faith and take this holy Sacrament to your comfort, and make your humble confession to Almighty God, meekly kneeling upon your knees.

Almighty God unto whom all hearts are open, all desires are known, and from whom no secrets are hid, cleanse the thoughts of our hearts by the inspiration of thy holy spirit, that we may perfectly love Thee and worthily magnify Thy holy name through Christ our Lord. Amen.

The Elder may add whatever he sees proper on the occasion.

The Elder shall then say the prayer of consecration, as followeth:

Almighty God our Heavenly Father, who of thy tender mercy didst give thine only Son, Jesus Christ, to suffer death upon the cross for our redemption, who made (by his oblation of himself once offered) a full, perfect and sufficient sacrifice, oblation and satisfaction for the sins of the whole world, and did institute and in His holy gospel command us to continue a perpetual memory of that precious death, until His coming again; hear us, O merciful Father, we most humbly beseech Thee, and grant that we, receiving these, Thy creatures of bread and wine, according to Thy Son, our Saviour Jesus Christ's holy institution, in remembrance of his death and passions, may be the partakers of his most blessed body and blood, who, in the same night that he was betrayed, took bread;*
and and when He had given thanks He break it* and gave it to His disciples, saying: Take, eat; this* is my body which is given for you; do this in remembrance of me. Likewise, after supper, He took*

* Here the Elder is to take the plate of bread into his hands.

* And here to break the bread.

* And here to lay his hands upon all the bread.

* Here he is to take the cup in his hands.

the cup; and when He had given thanks, He gave it to them, saying: Drink ye all of this, for this§

§ And here to lay his hands upon all vessels which contains the wine.

is my blood of the New Testament, which is shed for you, and for many, for the remission of sins: Do this as oft as ye shall drink this in remembrance of me. Amen.

Then shall the Minister first receive the Communion in both kinds himself, and then proceed to deliver the same to the other Ministers in like manner, (if any be present,) and after that to the people also in order, into their hands, and when he delivereth the bread he shall say:

The body of our Lord Jesus Christ, which was given for thee, preserve thy soul and body unto everlasting life. Take and eat this in remembrance that Christ died for thee, and feed on Him in thy heart by faith with thanksgiving.

And the Minister that delivereth the cup shall say:

The blood of our Lord Jesus Christ, which was shed for thee, preserve thy soul and body unto everlasting life. Drink this in remembrance that Christ's blood was shed for thee, and be thankful.

When all have communed, the Minister shall place upon the table, what remaineth of the elements, covering the same.

Then shall the Elder say the Lord's Prayer the people repeating after him every portion'

Our Father who art in heaven, hallowed be Thy name; Thy Kingdom come; Thy will be done on earth as it is in heaven; give us this day our daily bread, and forgive us our trespasses, as we forgive those that trespass against us; and lead us not into temptation, but deliver us from evil; for thine is the kingdom, the power, and the glory, for ever and ever. Amen.

The Elder, if he deem it expedient, may put up an extempore Prayer, and let the people depart with this blessing:

May the peace of God, which passeth all understanding, keep your hearts and minds in the knowledge and love of God, and his Son, Jesus Christ our Lord; and the blessing of God Almighty, the Father, the Son, and the Holy Ghost, be among you and remain with you always. Amen.

If the Elder be straitened for time, he may omit any part of the service, except the Prayer of Consecration:

BAPTISM OF INFANTS.

When the child to be Baptised is brought before the Minister, he shall say to the parents:

Beloved Friends:--You are about to dedicate your child to the service of the living and true God, who hath said : Behold, all souls are mine, as the soul of the Father, so also the soul of the Son is mine, and the promise of acceptance and salvation is to you and your children, and to all that are afar off. By this act you acknowledge the high claim of Almighty God to the life and services of your offspring to your infant, and to the Church of Christ, to guide its feet into the paths of righteousness, and to raise it up into the nature and admonition of the Lord.

You will need all the wisdom and grace to enable you to discharge this, your imperious duty, we therefore, exhort you to pray to God constantly, so to enlighten your minds, and influence your hearts, that you may both to precept and example, be enabled to lead your children in the true and right way, and induce them to glorify God, in their souls and bodies, which is their reasonable service.

Let us Pray.

Almighty and most merciful God, Father of Spirits, former of our Bodies, Redeemer and Saviour of our Souls, we thank thee that thou hast made it our privilege to dedicate our children to Thy service, that they may be lively members of the Church of Christ and heirs of eternal life.

We beseech thee, our heavenly Father, to bestow upon the parents of this child, grace whereby they may serve thee acceptably, with reverence and Godly fear in holiness and righteousness all the days of their lives, that by precept and example they may train their child in all Godly discipline and admonition, that it may be a worthy member of the Church of Christ. Grant, O Lord, that this child may die unto sin and live unto righteousness, and being steadfast in faith, joyful through hope and rooted in love, may safely pass the wave of this transitory life and finally come to the Heaven of eternal repose, there to dwell with thee world without end, through Jesus Christ our Lord.

Almighty God, grant that whosoever is dedicated to thee by our office and ministry, may be endowed with heavenly virtues and ever remain in the number of thy faithful children, and be made a partaker of eternal life through thy mercy, O blessed Lord God, who dost live and govern all things world without end. Amen.

The people shall stand up, and the minister shall say:

They brought young children to Christ that He should touch them, and His disciples rebuked those who brought them; but when Jesus saw it he was much displeased, and said. Suffer little children to come unto me and forbid them not, for of such is the Kingdom of God; verily I say unto you, whosoever shall not receive the Kingdom of God as a little child, shall not enter therein. And He took them up in His arms, put His hands upon them and blessed them.

The minister shall then take the child in his arms, and say to the friends of the child:

Name this child.

Repeating the name as given by the parents he shall say when baptizing:

N. I baptize thee in the name of the Father, and of the Son, and of the Holy Ghost. The Lord bless this child and grant him eternal life.

The minister shall then conclude with the apostolic benediction.

Infant baptism should be administered monthly in all our churches, and oftener, when necessary.

In infant baptism, let it be an invariable rule to require the attendance of the parents of the child.

Let every adult person, and the parents of every child to be baptized, have the choice of immersion, sprinkling or pouring.

Parents whose children have been baptized, should attend after service and inform the Minister of the age, etc., of the child or children baptized, that he may enter their ages, etc., on the Church register.

MINISTRATION OF BAPTISM TO SUCH AS ARE OF RIPER YEARS.

When the person to be baptised present themselves, the Minister shall say:

Dearly beloved: Forasmuch as all men are born in sin, and that our Saviour, Christ, saith none can enter the Kingdom of God except he be regenerated and born anew of water and of the Holy Ghost, I beseech you call upon God the Father, through our Lord Jesus Christ, that of His bounteous goodness He will grant to those persons now to be baptized, that which, by nature, they cannot have, and that they may be made lively members of the Church of Christ, and heirs of eternal life.

Let us Pray.

Almighty, everlasting God, whose most dearly beloved Son, Jesus Christ, for the forgiveness of our sins, did shed out of His most precious side both water and blood, and gave His commandment to His disciples that they should go and teach all nations, and baptize in the name of the Father, and of the Son, and of the Holy Ghost, regard, we beseech thee, the supplications of this congregation, and grant that the persons now to be baptized may receive the fullness of thy grace, and ever remain in the number of the elect children through Jesus Christ our Lord. O, merciful God, grant, through the sanctification of thy spirit and their belief of the truth as it is in Christ Jesus, that the carnal mind in them may be destroyed, and that they may be created anew in Christ Jesus unto good works, and have their fruit unto holiness and obtain everlasting life. Grant that they, being dedicated to thee by our office and ministry, receive grace whereby they may serve thee acceptably, with reverence and godly fear in holiness and righteousness, all the days of their lives, and being endowed with heavenly virtues, and strengthened by thy grace, may have victory, and be eventually rewarded through thy mercy, O, blessed Lord God, who dost live and govern all things. World without end, Amen.

The Minister shall demand of each of the persons to be baptised, severally:

1. Do you believe in the existence of God, and that He is a rewarder of those who diligently seek Him? I do.

2. Do you believe that the Lord Jesus Christ is the Redeemer and Saviour of the world? I do.

3. The sacred Scriptures inform us that we have all sinned and come short of the glory of God; but that if we confess our sins He is faithful and just to forgive our sins and to cleanse us from all unrighteousness. Are you now determined, by the aid of divine grace to forsake every evil way, to look to Christ as your only and all sufficient Saviour and to walk in all the commandments of God? I am.

4. It is made our duty to search the sacred Scriptures and to attend on all the ordinances of the house of God. Will you endeavor to be faithful in the discharge of these duties? I will, by the assistance of God's holy spirit.

The Minister shall then take each person to be Baptized by the right hand, shall ask the name and then repeating it sprinkle or pour water upon him, saying:

I baptize thee in the name of the Father and of the Son and of the Holy Ghost.

The Minister may then conclude with an extempore prayer. Repeat the Lord's Prayer and the Apostolical Benediction.

MARRIAGE CEREMONY.

At the day and time appointed for the solemnization of Matrimony, the persons to be married standing together, the man on the right hand and the woman on the left, the Minister shall say:

Dearly beloved: We are gathered together here in the sight of God, and in the presence of these witnesses, to join together this man and this woman in holy matrimony, which is an honorable estate, instituted of God in the days of man's innocency, signifying unto us the mystical union that is betwixt Christ and his Church, which holy estate Christ adorned and beautified with His presence, and the first miracle that He wrought in Cana of Galilee, and is recommended of St. Paul to be honorable among all men; and therefore, it is not by any to be dispised or taken in hand unadvisedly, but reverently, discretely, advisedly, and in fear of God. Into which holy estate these two present come now to be joined. Therefore if any one can show any just cause why they may not be lawfully joined together, let him now speak, or else hereafter forever hold his peace.

If no impediment be alleged, then shall the Minister say unto the man.

M. Wilt thou have this woman to be thy wedded wife, to live together, after God's ordinance, in the holy estate of matrimony? Wilt thou love her, comfort her, honor and keep her in sickness and in health, and forsaking all others keep thee only unto her so long as ye shall both live?

The man shall answer, I will

Then shall the Minister say unto the woman,

N. Wilt thou have this man to be thy wedded husband, to live together after God's ordinance in the holy estate of matrimony? Wilt thou obey him, serve him, love, honor and keep him, in sickness and in health, and forsaking all others, keep thee only to him so long as ye both shall live?

The woman shall answer, I will.

Then the minister shall cause the man with his right hand to take the woman by her right hand, and to repeat after him as followeth,

I, M, take thee, N, to be my wedded wife, to have and to hold, from this day forward, for better for worse, for richer for poorer, in sickness and in health, to love and to cherish, till death us do part, according to God's holy's ordinance, and therefore I plight thee my faith.

Then shall they loose their hands, and the woman, with her right hand, taking the man by his right hand, shall likewise say after the Minister,

I, N, take thee, M, to be my wedded husband, to have and to hold, from this day forward, for better for worse, for richer for poorer, in sickness and in health, to love, cherish and obey, till death do us part, according to God's holy ordinance, and thereto give thee my faith.

Then shall the Minister join their hands together and say,

Those whom God had joined together let no man put asunder.

Forasmuch as M and N have consented together in holy wedlock, and have witnessed the same before God and this company, and thereto pledged their faith, each to the other, and have declared the same by joining of hands, I pronounce that they are man and wife together, in the name of the Father and of the Son and of the Holy Ghost.

When the Minister shall add some wholesome advice and prayer suited to the occasion.

BURIAL OF THE DEAD.

The following or some other solemn service shall be used. The Minister meeting the corpse and going before it shall say:

I am the resurrection and the life, saith the Lord; he that believeth in me, though he were dead, yet shall he live; whosoever liveth and believeth in me shall never die.--John XI-25, 26.

I know that my Redeemer liveth, and that He shall stand at the latter day upon the earth, and though, after my skin, worms destroy this body, yet in my flesh shall I see God, whom I shall see for myself and mine eyes shall behold and not another.--Job XIX-25, 26, 27.

We brought nothing into this world, and it is certain we can carry nothing out; the Lord gave and the Lord hath taken away; blessed be the name of the Lord.

At the grave, when the corpse is laid in the earth the Minister shall say:

Man that is born of a woman hath but a short time to live, and is full of misery; he cometh up and is cut down like a flower, and never continueth in one stay.

In the midst of life we are in death; of whom may we seek for succor, but of thee, O Lord, who for our sins are justly displeased.

Yet, O Lord God most mighty, O holy and most merciful Saviour, deliver us not into the bitter pains of death eternal.

Thou knowest, Lord, the secrets of our hearts; shut not thy merciful ears to our prayers, but spare us, Lord most holy, O God most mighty, O holy and merciful Saviour, thou Most worthy Judge Eternal, suffer not at our last hour for any pains of death, to fall from thee.

Then while the earth is being cast on the body, the Minister shall say,

Forasmuch as it hath pleased Almighty God, in His wise Providence, to take out of this world the soul of our deceased brother, (or sister,) we therefore commit his (or her) body to the ground; earth to earth, ashes to ashes, dust to dust; looking for the general resurrection in the last day, and the life of the world to come through our Lord and Saviour Jesus Christ, at whose second coming, in glorious majesty, to judge the world, the earth and the sea shall give up their dead, and the corruptible bodies of those who sleep in Him shall be changed and made like unto His own glorious body, according to the mighty working whereby he is able to subdue all things unto himself.

I heard a voice from Heaven saying unto me: Write, from henceforth, blessed are the dead who die in the Lord; even so, saith the Spirit, for they rest from their labors.

Then shall the Minister say.

Lord have mercy upon us! Christ have mercy upon us! Lord have mercy upon us!

Our Father who art in Heaven, hallowed be thy name; thy Kingdom come; thy will be done on earth as it is in Heaven; give us this day our daily bread, and forgive us our trespasses as we forgive those that tresspass against us, and lead us not into temptation, but deliver us from evil, for thine is the Kingdom, the power and glory for ever and ever. Amen.

The Collect.

O merciful God, the Father of our Lord Jesus Christ, who is the resurrection and the life, in whom whosoever believeth shall live though he die, and whosoever liveth and believeth in Him shall not die eternally. We meekly beseech thee, O Father, to raise us from the death of sin unto righteousness, that when we shall depart this life we may rest in Him, and at the general resurrection on the last day may be found acceptable in thy sight, and receive that blessing which thy well beloved Son shall then pronounce to all that love and fear thee, saying: Come, ye blessed children of my Father; receive the Kingdom prepared for you from the beginning of the world. Grant this, we beseech thee, O, merciful Father, through Jesus Christ our Mediator and Redeemer. Amen.

The grace of our Lord Jesus Christ, and the love of God and the fellowship of the Holy Ghost be with us all evermore. Amen.

ORDAINING DEACONS.

On the day appointed for the ordination, an appropriate sermon or exhortation shall be delivered, after which one of the Ministers shall read aloud the names of those to be ordained deacons, who shall respectively answer and present themselves before the Ministers appointed to perform the ordination.

One of the Elders shall read the following passages,

Likewise must the Deacons be grave, not double-tongued, not given to much wine, not greedy of filthy lucre; holding the mystery of the faith in a pure conscience. And let these also first be proved, then let them use the office of Deacon, being found blameless. Even so must their wives be grave, not slanderous, sober, faithful in all things[.] Let the Deacons be the husbands of one wife, ruling their children and their own house well. For they who have used the office of Deacon well, purchase to themselves a good degree and great boldness in the faith which is in Christ Jesus.

Let another of the Elders say to the persons about to be ordained.

Do you trust that you are inwardly moved by the Holy Ghost to take upon you the office of the Ministry in the Church of Christ? to serve God for the promoting of His glory and the edifying of His people?

A. I trust so.

Beloved brethren: Forasmuch as the Holy Scriptures command that we should not be hasty in lying on hands and admitting persons to minister in the Church of Christ; therefore, before we admit you to the office of a Deacon in the Church of God, we will examine you in the presence of this congregation, and receive your answers to the following questions:

Are you fully persuaded that the Holy Scriptures contain sufficiently all doctrine required of necessity for eternal salvation? and will you out of the same Holy Scriptures, instruct the people, and teach, and maintain nothing as of necessity required for salvation, but that which you shall be persuaded may be proved by them?

Will you faithfully exercise yourself in the study of the Holy Scriptures, and call upon God by prayer for the true understanding of the same, so that you may be able to teach and exhort with wholesome doctrine, and to stand and convince gainsayers?

Will you deny all ungodliness and worldly lust, and live soberly, righteously and godly in this world, that you may show yourself in all things a worthy example to the flock of Christ?

Will you diligently endeavor to teach and discipline your family according to the doctrine of the Gospel, and make them as much as in you lieth, example to others?

Will you strive to maintain quietness peace and love among all Christian people, and especially among them who are committed to your care?

Let us Pray.

Almighty God, giver of every good and perfect gift, mercifully behold these, thy servants, now set apart for the office work of Deacons in thy Church; grant so to replenish them with the truth of thy doctrine and adorn them with innocence of life, that both by word and good example they may faithfully serve the Church in this office to the glory of thy name and the edification of thy people through the merits of our Saviour Jesus Christ Amen

The Elders present shall then lay their hands severally upon the head of every one that receiveth the order of Deacon, the receivers remaining on their knees for the convenience of the ordainers; the President pronouncing the following words,

The Lord pour upon thee the Holy Spirit for the office and work of a Deacon, committed unto thee by the election of thy brethren, and the imposition of our hands.

Be thou faithful. Give heed unto reading, exhortation and doctrine. Be diligent, that thy advancement in grace and knowledge may be manifest unto all men, and that thou mayest save thyself and those that hear thee.

The President shall then deliver to every one of them the Bible in his hands saying,

We acknowledge thy authority to preach this word, and to assist the Elder in the administration of the ordinances in the Church of God.

We charge thee before God and the Lord Jesus Christ, who shall judge the quick and the dead, preach the word; be instant in season, out of season; reprove, rebuke, exhort with all long suffering and doctrine.

Then shall the President say.

Let us Pray.

Most merciful Father, we beseech thee to grant unto these, thy servants now set apart to the office of Deacon, thy blessing, and so endue them with thy holy spirit that they, preaching thy word, may not only be earnest to reprove, beseech and exhort with all patience and long suffering, but also may to such as believe, wholesome examples in doctrine, in conversation, in love, in faith, in charity, in purity, that, faithfully fulfilling their course, at the last day each may receive a crown of righteousness, laid up by the Lord, the righteous Judge who liveth and reigneth, one God with the Father, Son and Holy Ghost--world without end.

Assist us, O, Lord, in all our doings, with thy most gracious favor, and further us with thy continued help, that in all our works, begun, continued and ended in thee, we may glorify thy holy name, and finally, by thy mercy, obtain everlasting life through Jesus Christ our Lord. Amen.

FORM AND MANNER OF ORDAINING ELDERS.

On the day of ordination, a sermon or exhortation shall be delivered, after which one of the elders shall read aloud the names of the persons to be ordained, who shall answer respectively, and present themselves before the Ministers appointed to perform the ordination.

One of the Elders shall read the following passages of Holy Writ:

And Jesus came and spake unto them, saying: All power is given unto me in Heaven and in earth; go ye therefore and teach all nations, baptising them in the name of the Father, and of the Son, and of the Holy Ghost. Teaching them to observe all things whatsoever I command you, and lo, I am with you always, even unto the end of the world. Amen. --Matt. XXVIII-18, 20.

But unto every one of us is given grace according to measure of the gift of Christ; wherefore he saith, when he ascended up on high he led captivity captive, and gave gifts unto men. Now that he ascended, what is it but that he also descended, first into the lower parts of the earth. He that descended is the same also that ascended up far above all heavens, that he might fill all things; and he gave some apostles, and some prophets, and some evangelists, and some pastors and teachers; for the perfecting of the Saints, for the working of the Ministry, for the edifying of the body of Christ, till we all come in the unity of the faith, and of the knowledge of the Son of God, unto a perfect man, unto the measurer of the statue of the fullness of Christ.--Eph. iv-7, 13.

This is a true saying: If a man desireth an office in the Church of Christ, he desireth a good work. Then let the Elders that rule well be counted worthy of double honors, especially they who labor in the word and doctrine--1 Tim. v. 17. An Elder then must be blameless, the husband of one wife, vigilent, and sober, of good behavior, given to hospitality, apt to teach, not given to wine, no striker, not greedy of filthy lucre, but patient, not a brawler, nor covetous; one that ruleth well his own house, having his children in subjection with gravity. For if a man know not how to rule his own house, how shall he take care of the church of God? Not a novice, lest being lifted up with pride, he fall into the condemnation of the devil. Moreover, he must have a good report of them which are without, lest he fall into reproach and the snare of the devil.--1 Tim. 1, 7.

Another of the Elders shall say to the persons about to be ordained,

Beloved brethren: Forasmuch as the Holy Scriptures command that we should not be hasty in laying on of hands and admitting persons to Minister in the Church of Christ; therefore, before we admit you to the office of Elder in the

Church of God, we will examine you in the presence of this congregation, and receive your answers to the following questions:

Are you fully persuaded that the Holy Scriptures contain all doctrines required of necessity for eternal salvation? and will you, out of the same Holy Scriptures, instruct the people, and teach and maintain nothing as of necessity required for salvation, but that which you shall be persuaded may be proved by them yourself.

Will you faithfully exercise in the study of the Holy Scriptures, and call upon God by prayer for the true understanding of the same, so that you may be able to teach and exhort with wholesome doctrine, and to withstand and convince gainsayers?

Will you deny all ungodliness and worldly lust, and live soberly, righteously and godly in this present world, that you may show yourself in all things a worthy example to the flock of Christ?

Will you diligently endeavor to teach and discipline your family according to the doctrine of the gospel, and make them as much as in you lieth, examples to others?

Will you strive to maintain quietness, peace and love, among all Christian people, and especially among them who are committed to your care?

Let us pray.

All shall now kneel before God, and the Elder shall say[,]

Almighty God, giver of every good and perfect gift, mercifully behold these, thy servants, now set apart for the office and work of Elders in thy church; grant so to replenish them with the truth of thy doctrine, and adorn them with innocency of life, that both by word and good example, they may faithfully serve the Church in this office, to the glory of Thy name, and the edification of thy people, through the merits of our Saviour Jesus Christ. Amen

The Elders present shall then lay their hands severally upon the head of every one that receiveth the order of Elders, the receivers remaining on their knees for the convenience of the ordainers; the President pronouncing aloud the following words:

The Lord pour upon thee the Holy Spirit for the office and work of an Elder, committed unto thee by the election of thy brethren and the imposition of our hands, and be thou faithful.

The President shall then deliver to each one of them the Bible in his hands, saying:

We acknowledge thy authority to preach this word, and to administer the ordinances in the Church of Christ.

Feed the flock of God, taking the oversight thereof, not as a Lord over God's heritage, but being an example to the flock; and when the Chief Shepherd shall appear, thou shalt receive a crown of glory that fadeth not away.

Then shall the President say,

Let us pray.

Most merciful Father, we beseech thee to grant unto thy servants, now set apart to the office of Elder, thy heavenly blessing, and so endow them with Thy Holy Spirit, that they, preaching Thy word, may not only be earnest to reprove, beseech and exhort, with all patience and long suffering, but also may be such as believe wholesome examples in doctrine, in conversation, in love, in faith, in charity, that faithfully fulfilling their course, at the last day; each one may receive a crown of righteousness, laid up by the Lord, the righteous judge who liveth and reigneth, one God with the Father, Son and Holy Ghost, world without end.

Assist us, O Lord, in all our doings, with thy most gracious favor, and further us with thy continued help, that in all our works, begun, continued and ended in Thee, we may glorify thy holy name, and finally, by thy mercy, obtain everlasting life through Jesus Christ our Lord. Amen.

Benediction.

The peace of God which passeth all understanding, keep your hearts and minds in the love of God and of His Son, Jesus Christ, our Lord, and the blessing of God Almighty, the Father, the Son and the Holy Ghost, be with you always. Amen.

FORMULA FOR LAYING CORNER STONES, AND THE DEDICATION OF CHURCHES,

This ceremony should be preceded or followed by the delivery of an ap
ropriate discourse. The officers and memb rs of the congregation being present,
the services are introduced by singing a suitable hymn, If the discourse has not
been pronounced, the following prayer may be used.

Prayer.

Supremely great and glorious Jehovah, who art the King eternal, immortal
and invisible, the only wise God, to whom belong honor and glory, for ever and
ever! Thou fillest all space with thy presence, pervading universal nature, and
manifesting thy perfections in all thy works. We desire to approach thee in deep
humility, and in the exercise of living faith. We rejoice that, through Jesus
Christ, our Mediator and Redeemer, we have access to thy throne of grace, and
are taught to call thee *our* God, and to worship thee as our reconciled Father. We
thank thee for permitting us to assemble on the present occasion, amid
circumstances of so much mercy, to lay the corner-stone of an edifice which is to
be reared to thy honor, and to be dedicated to the exclusive worship of the true
and living God, Father, Son and Holy Ghost. We earnestly beseech thee to draw
nigh to us, as a God of love, and bless us with thy special presence. May the
object that has called us together be acceptable to thee, and may the solemnities
of this joyful and interesting occasion meet with thy sanction and be attended by
thy blessing. While we devoutly acknowledge our dependence upon thee, as well
in our attempt to erect a house for thy worship, as in the prosecution of the object
for which it is intended, we pray thee that no unholy desire may find place in our
breast, that all our motives may be pure, and that our great aim may be the
promotion of thy glory, the conversion of sinners, and the edification of thy
people in the truth as it is in Christ. May we obtain favor in thy sight, and may
thy rich mercy be upon us. Pardon our sins, help our infirmities, and accept our
prayer, through the merits of Jesus Christ, our adorable Saviour. And to thee, the
Triune God, be all praise, now and ever-more. Amen.

[Here a suitable portion of Scripture may be read; for instance, the 96th
Psalm, or 1 Cor. 3d chap., or 1 Kings, 5th chap, or Haggai, 1st chap., from 1-10
ver.

If the discourse has been preached, then the preceding prayer may be omitted; also, if deemed necessary, the Scripture lesson; and the exercises, after an appropriate hymn, may be continued with the following address.

Beloved brethren: Believing it to be your duty, as well as privilege, to worship God in a public and social capacity, and impressed with the conviction that the interests of Christ's kingdom and the salvation of souls may be thereby promoted, you have resolved, in reliance on God's blessing, to erect an edifice for the purpose of public worship, and are now assembled to lay the corner-stone. Though there is no specific law of God expressly requiring this at your hands, yet you justly infer from general principles laid down in the Sacred Scriptures, as well as from the dictates of enlightened reason, that it is your duty; and hence you do well in uniting for the accomplishment of a work so important, and holding forth the promise of so much good to yourselves and your descendents. We trust you are actuated by motives which God approves, and that you sincerely love Zion, and can truly adopt the language of the devout Psalmist: "How amiable are thy tabernacles, O Lord of hosts! My soul longeth, yea, even fainteth, for the courts of the Lord."

We find frequent allusions in God's word to the *corner-stone.* "Behold," says the Lord, in Isaiah: ["]I lay in Zion, for a foundation, a stone, a tried stone, a precious corner-stone, a sure foundation: he that believeth shall not make haste." And, in the Epistle to the Ephesians, the Apostle remarks: "Being built upon the foundation of the Apostles and Prophets, Jesus Christ being the chief corner-stone." Thus it appears that the corner-stone was a part of the *foundation* on which the edifice rested--Having its place in the corner, it united and bound together two walls. One corner-stone was laid upon another; and the same was done at each of the four corners of the building. The corner-stones were, therefore many; but all of them, taken collectively, were spoken of as *one.* A single stone, larger, stronger, and more beautiful than the others, was laid in one of the corners, either at the top or the bottom of the foundation wall, as the representative of all the rest, and of the whole foundation; and was emphatically termed *the* corner-stone, the chief corner stone, or the head of the corner. Hence Jesus Christ is called both the *foundation* and the *corner-stone,* in the stupendous edifice of Christianity. By which is meant, that He is the support and strength of His Church, preserving it firm and unshaken, and extending its borders till it shall encompass the earth; that He unites and binds together its members by the cords of that love which forms the strongest of all incentives to harmony of feeling and action; and that He is also the glory of the Church, both because of the elevating and sanctifying influences of His doctrines on the moral character of His followers, and on account of His supreme personal excellence He is, therefore, most appropriately denominated 'a chief corner stone, elect, precious," sustaining the whole system, and without which Christianity would cease to be Christianity, and soon fall to the ground.

By laying the corner stone of a house of worship, you perform a decisive act; you publicly announce that a commencement is made to build the house, and that it is your determination, by the help of God, to complete it. This decisive act, so full of promise, and waking up emotions and prospects so pleasing and joyful, is justly made a prominent one, and accompanied by solemnities suited to the occasion, and adapted to inspire us with an abiding sense of God's goodness, and our insufficiency without Him. It is right and proper that we should publicly acknowledge our dependence on Him, both in the attempt to erect an edifice, and in the discharge of the solemn duties for which it is intended.

Such an acknowledgment gives to God an honor which is due to Him, and at the same time impresses our hearts with reverence and awe towards Him. "Except the Lord build the house, they labor in vain who build it." This was the sentiment of Solomon, the wisest and the richest of the kings of Israel, whose prosperity in all his great undertakings was so remarkable, and brought so much glory to his reign. It becomes us, like him, on all occasions, especially in every important matter, to be deeply sensible of the power, the universal dominion, the all-wise, holy and irresistible government of God; to feel that we are His needy creatures, and dependent on His pleasure for each moment of our existence; that the success of all our exertions is the result of His blessing; and that when we design to honor him, or to promote the public good, it is for *Him* to say whether we are the instruments and *our measures* the means which he will choose to employ for those ends. When David contemplated the erection of a house of God, the Lord forbade him, and said, "I have chosen thy son to build me a house."

Let us therefore humble ourselves before the Lord, confess His name, and seek His blessing in fervent prayer.

Prayer.

O thou, whom the Heaven of Heavens cannot contain! Thou fillest the universe with Thy presence, and all the praise of angels and men can add nothing to thy majesty and glory. But though thou needest not our worship, we adore

Thee that thou art too good to despise it, and that millions have experienced that thou art a prayer-hearing and a prayer answering God. We rejoice that thou has established thy church here on earth, and preserved the same against all assaults of its enemies; that the blessed sound of the gospel has also saluted our ears, and that thou hast in this place gathered a congregation of believers in Jesus Christ.

We render thanks unto thy name that Thou hast put it into the hearts of Thy people to rear a temple to thine honor at this place, where thy name may be regarded, and Thou mayest come to them and bless them. We extol Thy grace for enduing them with a spirit of liberality, and inclining them to contribute of their substance to prosecute this laudable undertaking. May they indeed esteem it a high privilege to lend unto the Lord, and may many others co-operate in this holy work, and all labor together in concord and love until the habitation of thy house shall be completed and held in possession free from debt and all incumbrance, as a standing memorial of their Christian benevolence, and an evidence to future generations of their attachment to Thy cause. May the work of this house be performed without hurt or accident to any person; may harmony and enlightened zeal animate every heart, and may discord, jealousy and every selfish aim be far removed. And when thou shalt have prospered this enterprise, and a house of God shall stand here as a monument to thy glory, may it be filled with the fulness of every gospel blessing; that through the preaching of thy truth, many blood-bought souls may here be awakened, enlightened, justified and sanctified, and thus be prepared for an entrance into the mansions of bliss. We beseech thee to seal unto us the pardon of all our offences, to own us as thy ransomed people through Jesus Christ, to sanctify us thoroughly by thy spirit, to guide us through life by thy counsels, to secure us by thy grace, and to exalt us at last to an inheritance that is incorruptible, undefiled, and that fadeth not away. These and all other' needful blessings we ask for the sake and in the name of our Lord Jesus Christ, to whom with the Father and Holy Spirit be endless praise. Amen.

The preceding prayer, or any other suitable one having been offered, the stone shall be laid and adjusted. The officiating minister deposits the documents in the excavation prepared in the stone for their reception. These documents may be the articles of subscription and names of their subscribers; a list of the church officers, the pastor and building committee, and of the ministers officiating on the occasion, the Discipline of the Church, Hymn Book, Bible, the names of the highest officers of Government, religious papers of the Church &c., &c. The Minister then concludes with the following declaration:

In the name of the Triune God, the Father and Son and Holy Spirit, we lay this stone for a foundation of a house of worship to be consecrated to His service. In so doing we acknowledge His all-ruling Providence, and proclaim Jesus Christ as the great corner-stone of His church, and the foundation of all our hopes of salvation in time and eternity; and may the God of all grace hear us, sanction our work, and at last accept us, through the Son of His love, our only Lord and Saviour. Amen.

FORMULA FOR THE DEDICATION OF NEW OR RE-MODELLED CHURCHES.

The President, or Elder, (when the Prsident is not present,) when the other Ministers, shall be met at the door of the Church by the Trustees, Steward and Leaders, who shall receive the President, or Elder, with the Ministers, and bid them welcome in God's name, and present to the President or Elder the keys of the Church in token of the fact that they will ever after submit to the Discipline, doctrine and government of the African Union First Colored Methodist Protestant Church, and "will at all times hereafter permit such Ministers and Preachers belonging to said Church to preach and expound God's Holy Word therein." After which the procession shall pass up the aisle reading the following Psalm[.] The President or Elder commencing with the first verse, and the Minister reading each alternate verse.

PSALM LXXXIV.

President-- How amiable are thy tabernacles, O Lord of hosts!

Minister.--My soul longeth, yea, even fainteth for the courts of the Lord: my heart and my flesh crieth out for the living God.

Prest--Yea, the sparrow hath found a house, and the swallow a nest for yourself, where she may lay her young, even thine altars, O Lord of hosts, my King and my God.

Min.--Blessed are they that dwell in thy house: they will be still praising thee.

Prest--Blessed is the man whose strength is in thee; in whose hearts are the ways of them.

Min.--Who passing through the valley of Baca make it a well: the rain also filleth the pools.

Prest.--They go from strength to strength; every one of them in Zion appeareth before God.

Min.--O Lord God of hosts, hear my prayer: give ear, O God of Jacob.

Prest--Behold, O God, our Shield, and look upon the face of thine anointed.

Min.--For a day in thy courts is better than a thousand. I had rather be a door-keeper in the house of my God, than to dwell in the tents of wickedness.

Prest.--For the Lord God is a sun and shield; the Lord will give grace and glory; no good thing will He withhold from them that walk uprightly.

Min--O Lord of hosts, blessed is the man that trusteth in thee.

The President,*

* Or Elder.

with those who are appointed to lead the exercises, will now take their seats in the pulpit, the rest of the clergy sitting around it, and the choir will chant the following--

PSALM CXXII.

1. I was glad when they said unto me, Let us go into the House of the Lord.

2. Our feet shall stand within thy gates, O Jerusalem.

3. Jerusalem is builded as a city that is compact together.

4. Whither the tribes go up, the tribes of the Lord, unto the testimony of Israel, to give thanks unto the name of the Lord.

5. For there are set thrones of judgment, the thrones of the house of David.

6. Pray for the peace of Jerusalem; they shall prosper that love thee.

7. Peace be within thy walls, and prosperity within thy palaces.

8. For my brethren and companions' sakes, I will now say, Peace be within thee.

9. Because of the house of the Lord our God, I will seek thy good.

The President,*

* Or Elder.

kneeling, shall then say the following prayer,

1 KINGS VIII. 23-51.

Lord God of Israel, there is no God like thee in Heaven above, or earth beneath, who keepest covenant and mercy with thy servants that walk before thee with all their heart: but will God indeed dwell on the earth? behold, the heaven of heavens cannot contain thee; how much less this house that we have builded? Yet have thou respect unto the prayer of thy servants, and to their supplications, O Lord our God, to hearken unto the cry and the prayer which thy servants pray before thee this day: that thine eyes may be open towards this house, night and day, even toward the place of which thou hast said, My name shall be there: that thou mayest hearken unto the prayer which thy servants shall make in this place. And hearken thou unto the supplication of thy servants, and of thy people Israel, when they shall pray in this place; and hear thou in Heaven, thy dwelling place; and when thou hearest, forgive. If any man trespass against his neighbor, and an accusation be laid against him, and the accusation come before thee in this house--then hear thou in heaven, and do, and judge thy servants, condemning the wicked, to bring his way upon his head; and justifying the righteous, to give him according to his righteousness. When thy people, Israel, be smitten down before the enemy because they have sinned against thee, and shall turn again to thee, and confess thy name, and pray, and make supplication unto thee in this house--then hear thou in heaven, and forgive the sins of thy people Israel, and restore them again to *thy tender mercy and loving kindness.* When Heaven is shut up, and there is no rain, because they have sinned against thee; if they pray in this place, and confess thy name and turn from their sin, when thou afflictest them, then hear thou in heaven and forgive the sin of thy servants, and of thy people Israel, that thou teach them the good way wherein they should walk, and give rain upon the land which thou hast given to thy people for an inheritance. If there be in the land famine, if there be pestilence, blasting, mildew, locust, or if there be caterpillar; if their enemy besiege them in the land of their cities; whatsoever plague, whatsoever sickness there be; what prayer and supplication soever be made by any man, or by all thy people Israel, which shall know every man the plague of his own heart, and spread forth his hands in this house--then hear thou in Heaven, thy dwelling place, and forgive and do, and give to every man according to his ways, whose heart thou knowest; that they may fear thee all the days *of their lives.* Moreover, concerning a stranger, that is not of thy people, Israel, but cometh out of a far country for thy name's sake; when he shall come and pray within this house; hear thou in heaven, thy dwelling place, and do according to all that the stranger calleth to thee for; that all the people of the earth may know thy name, to fear thee, as do thy people Israel; and that they may know that this house, which we have builded, is called by thy name. If thy people sin against thee, for there is no man that sinneth not, and thou be angry with them, yet, if they shall bethink themselves and repent, and make supplication unto thee, saying: We have sinned and done perversely, we have committed wickedness; and so return unto thee with all their heart, and with all their soul; then hear thou their prayer and supplication in Heaven, thy dwelling-place, and forgive thy people that have sinned against thee, and all their transgressions wherein they have transgressed against thee, for they be thy people and thy inheritance, *which thou hast bought with the precious blood of thy Son, Jesus Christ, our Lord; to whom with thee and the Holy Spirit, be glory, praise and power, by all on earth, and all in heaven. Amen.*

This prayer being over, the President or Elder shall stand up and say,

And now, O Lord God, most high, whom the heaven and heaven of heavens cannot contain, we dedicate this house to thy service; receive it, we humbly beseech thee, receive it unto thyself, and number it among thine earthly sanctuaries; that thine own presence, the presence of thy Son, Jesus Christ, and the presence of thy Holy Spirit, may ever fill this house which we have builded and called by thy name, so that whensoever the Gospel is preached in this house, it may descend with all its purity, power and demonstration, upon the hearts of the impenitent, turning them from darkness to light, and from the power of sin and Satan, unto God; that its sanctifying influences may be felt in the souls of all believers, lifting their desires, their hopes and their affections, from earth to heaven, and leading back the wandering sheep of the house of Israel into the fold of eternal life. Amen.

Hear us, O merciful Father, and grant that whosoever shall be dedicated to thee in this house by the holy ordinance of baptism, they may also receive the fullness of thy grace, be made useful members of the church militant, and finally obtain an abundant entrance into the church triumphant, through Jesus Christ our Lord. Amen.

Hear us, O merciful Father, and grant that whosoever shall in this house partake of the symbols of the Saviour's broken body and shed blood, may also realize, by faith, that He is indeed the Lamb of God that taketh away the sin of the world; and thus being regenerated and sanctified, stand spotless and life-crowned at thy right hand, world without end. Amen.

Hear us, O Thou who art the Spouse of the Church, and grant that whosoever shall in this house be joined together in holy matrimony, may also live, as did Isaac and Rebecca, in the purest enjoyment of connubial love, mutually assisting each other in the way to Heaven, and training up their children for usefulness in this life, and for glory in that which is to come, through Jesus Christ our Lord. Amen.

O thou high and holy one of Israel, regard, we beseech thee, the prayers of thy servants, and grant that all who shall, in this house, make confession of their sins, or lift their voices in praise and thanksgiving for mercies past or benefits received, may also rejoice in the light of thy countenance, with the peace which passeth all understanding; with the joy that is unspeakable and full of glory.-- Amen.

Great Head of the Church, we beseech thee to hear us, and grant that whosoever shall, in this house, be set apart or ordained to the holy office of the ministry, may also receive the anointing of thy Spirit, and go forth in the fulness of the blessing of the Gospel, to preach its unsearchable riches to a ruined world; then, having finished their course, fought the fight, and kept the faith, receive the crown of life and reign with thee, world without end. Amen.

Thou God of missions, hear us, and grant that the sacred cause of missions, with every other institution of Christianity, may ever find in this house an able advocacy and an ample support, so as to be rendered instrumental in hastening on the day when the kingdoms this world shall have become the kingdom of our Lord and his Christ. Amen.

FORMS OF CREDENTIALS, LICENSES, CERTIFICATES, &C.

Form of a License to Exhort.

A---- B----, a member of the African Union First Colored Methodist Protestant Church, residing in the ---- Station, is hereby authorized to exercise himself on all proper occasion in exhortation, and calling sinners to repentance. This license to be renewed annually.

Signed by order and in behalf of the Quarterly Conference of ----.

January ----, 18--.

> E---- F----, Chairman.
> C----D----, Secretary.

Form of a License to Preach.

C---- D----, a member of the African Union First Colored Methodist Protestant Church, residing in ---- Circuit being duly examined by this Quarterly Conference, on gifts, grace and acquirements, is hereby authorized to preach the gospel of Christ. This license to be renewed annually.

Signed by order and in behalf of the Quarterly Conference of ----.

January ----, 18--.

> J---- K----, Chairman.
> G---- H----, Secretary.

Form of Deacon's Credentials.

To all whom it may concern, greeting:--

Be it known, That A---- B----, having been duly recommended, and having been elected by the ---- Annual Conference of Ministers and Delegates, was ordained for the office of Deacon in the African Union First Colored Methodist Protestant Church, and is hereby authorized by said Conference to baptize, to assist the Elder in the administration of the Lord's Supper, to celebrate matrimony, and to preach and expound the Holy Scriptures so long as his life and doctrine accord with the gospel of our Lord Jesus Christ.

Signed by order and in behalf of the ---- Annual Conference.

January ----, 18--.

S---- T----, President.
T---- K----, Secretary.

Form of Elders Credentials.

To all whom it may concern, greeting:--

Be it known, That C---- D----, having been elected by the Annual Conference of Ministers and Delegates, was ordained for the office of Elder, in the African Union First Colored Methodist Protestant Church ; and he is hereby authorized by said Conference, so long as his life and doctrine accord with the Holy Scriptures, to administer the Lord's Supper, to baptize, to celebrate matrimony, and to feed the flock of God, taking the oversight, not as a lord over God's heritage, but being an example to the flock.

Signed by order, and in behalf of the

---- Annual Conference.

January --, 18 ___.

N---- S----, President.
A---- C----, Secretary.

Form of Certificate of Membership.

The bearer hereof, T---- W----, an acceptable member of the African Union First Colored Methodist Protestant Church, being desirous of removing from this Station, is entitled to receive from the undersigned this certificate of his good standing.

B---- Station, Jan. ----, 18--.

W---- G----, Minister.

Form of Certificate for an unstationed Minister or Preacher, who desires to remove to another Circuit, Station or District.

The bearer, S---- B----, an unstationed Minister of the African Union First Colored Methodist Protestant Church, being desirous of removing from this Circuit, is entitled to receive from the undersigned, this certificate of his good standing.

F---- Circuit, Jan. ----, 18--.

W---- P----, Minister.

Form of a Certificate for a Stationed Minister or Preacher, who desires to remove to another District.

The bearer, J---- L----, having fully complied with his engagements to the ---- Annual Conference, his moral character standing fair, and being desirous of removing to another District is entitled to this Certificate of his good standing.

January ----, 18--.

A---- S----,
Pres't of the M---- Annual Conference.

Form of Transfer.

The bearer, A---- S----, of the O---- Annual Conference having consented to be transferred to the M---- Annual Conference, is hereby duly transferred.

January --, 18 --.

C---- S----, Pres't of the O---- Annual Conference.

E---- H----, Pres't of the M---- Annual Conference.

Form of Certificate of Election.

This is to certify that A---- B---- was duly elected to the Annual Conference of the ---- District, to sit in ----, on the ---- day of ----, 18--, by the ----, of the ----.

A---- B----, Chairman.
S---- P----, Secretary.

Form of Certificates of Election.

A---- B---- was duly elected by the Electoral College of the M---- District, held on ---- day of ----, 18--, a Ministerial Representative to the General Conference of the African Union First Colored Methodist Protestant Church, to sit in the city of ----, on the ---- day of ----, 18--.

G---- H----, Chairman.
P---- S----, Secretary.

E---- F----, was duly elected by the Electoral College of the M---- District, held on this ---- day of ---- 18--, a Lay Representative to the General Conference of the African Union First Colored Methodist Protestant Church, to sit in ---- city, on the ---- day of ----, 18--.

G---- H----, Chairman.
P---- S----, Secretary.

APPENDIX.

Amendments to different Articles.

The General Conference shall have power to create a Foreign and Home Mission, and to make rules and regulations for the same. It shall be the duty of the Foreign Missionaries to report to the nearest Annual Conference.

OF CONSTITUTING CLASS LEADERS.

The Class Leaders shall be nominated by the official Board, and elected by the members of each class; and if any member should become dissatisfied in their class, or the time of meeting not be convenient for them, and the same desire to be transferred to another class, if they show satisfactory reasons for such changes, the Minister may grant the same.

TRANSFER FROM ONE DISTRICT TO ANOTHER.

The Presidents of each District shall have the power, by mutual agreement, to transfer any brother to another District in the interval of the Annual Conference.

First, by giving two months' notice to the one to be transferred; *Provided,* the brother will accept the appointment.

Each Annual Conference shall have power in the several Districts to transfer any one of their members from one District to another, with the consent of the brother.

DUTY OF ELDERS HAVING THE SUPERVISION.

It shall be the duty of an Elder having the supervision of a traveling Preacher or Deacon, to administer the Sacrament of the Lord's Supper; to assist them occasionally in the Quarterly Conference, or in settling any difficulty arising in their charge.

RELIEF FUND.

The General Conference recommend that all of our Ministers going on a charge take up a public collection once or twice in their charge during the Conference year, for the support of our worn out Preachers. The Minister's Steward shall hold said moneys until the ensuing Annual Conference, and pay the same over to order to that body.

GENERAL CLASS MEETINGS.

There shall be a General Class Meeting held in this Connection the week previous to the Quarterly Meetings, and each member shall receive their Love Feast tickets, and pay their quarterage at said meeting.

MISSIONARIES.

Foreign Missionaries shall be members of the General Conference, and Home Missionaries shall be subject to the nearest Quarterly Conference in the Circuit or Station.

The General Conference recommend that all the Churches in the Connection take up a public collection every quarter for the support of the missionary cause, and the moneys so collected be deposited in the Home Mission Fund.

It shall be the duty of each member to pay the stipulated sum of three cents a quarter for the support of the Foreign Missionaries, and the same deposited in said fund.

DENOMINATED FUNDS.

First, the President Fund, and shall be held by the Stewards of each station or circuits.

Second shall be denominated Home Mission Fund, said fund to be held by the Stewards.

Third, Relief Fund for the superannuated, worn out Preachers, held by the Stewards appointed for that purpose.

Fourth, Foreign Mission Fund, shall be denominated as such, and shall be held by the Steward of each station or circuit, whose duty it shall be to report to each Quarterly Conference, and to pay over to the Official Board when demanded.

BIGAMY AND IMPROPER MARRIAGES.

1. Any preacher or member that do marry and afterwards separate without a lawful cause, and marries any one else, shall be expelled from our connexion.-- Any minister, preacher or member so expelled, shall not be priviledged to join our church again until they have abandoned the intimacy so existing.

2. Any minister, preacher or member marrying any woman that has became separated from her lawful husband without a lawful cause, shall be expelled.

3. And any woman member marrying a man who has became separated from his lawful wife without a cause shall be expelled, and in either of the above cases shall not be taken in church until they abandon the evil.

RECEPTION OF OTHER PREACHERS.

All preachers or ministers coming from other denominations, that are in good standing in their respective churches, may be priviledged to preach in our churches.

THE TEMPORAL CONCERNS OF OUR CHURCHES.

1. The temporal concerns of our churches shall be governed by trustees or stewards, according to the charters or constitutions of the different societies of our connexion.

2. And all the churches shall elect their trustees according to the laws of their States in which the church is located.

ECONOMY OF THE CONNEXION.

Whereas, we the General Conference see the great necessity of sustaining our connexion, by supporting the General Conference, therefore

Resolved, That we do hereby recommend to all of our members throughout the connexion to give liberal in support of said object, and it shall be the duty of the minister having charge to instruct his people in time, to collect monies for the above object, so that we will not have to beg so much when the General Conference is in session.

GENERAL RULES.

1. The minister in charge shall have power to change improper class-leaders.

2. The ministers in charge shall appoint his Stewards agreeable to the Trustees and official board of his circuit or station, in his first Quarterly Conference.

3. Any brother that has been raised up in our church and makes application for license can be received; if after six months probation he sustains his examination. He shall be licensed after one year.

4. Any brother coming from another connexion, and not being properly recommended, shall not be licensed to preach or exhort until he has been a member for one year, and stood out their examination.

5. The duty of a preacher Stewards is to provide the elements for the Lord's Supper and love feast, and pay over all monies that he has received from the leaders for the ministers in charge and the President of the district, and for missionaries or relief, whenever ordered by the official board, and take a receipt for the same, and make his report quarterly and annually to the Conferences.

6. It shall be the duty of the church Stewards, either of stations or circuits to keep a fair and accurate account of all monies collected in the said church, and all the doings, temporal transactions by the trustees or official board, and make his report to the Quarterly.

7. It shall be the duty of each class leader in circuit or station to keep a book of all monies that he has received from his class for the president or minister in charge and record the names of all of his members that has paid their tithes, and any leader failing to discharge this important duty, it shall be considered an act of

neglect and he shall be brought to trial by the official board, and if found guilty shall have his class taken from him.

8. Any minister or preacher coming from another denomination to join Conference, must remain on trial one year before being admitted to full membership.

9. No preacher shall be eligible to Deacon's orders until he has traveled two years in this connexion, and no Deacon shall be eligible to Elder's orders until he has travelled two years, without extreme necessity, in such case the Annual Conference may ordain him.

10. The President of each district in the interval of the Annual Conference shall have power with three other Elders or more to perform an ordination when circumstances make it needful.

11. And it shall be the duty of all Stewards holding monies for the Annual Conference to forward it by the delegate or otherwise.

RECOMMENDATION.

The General Conference do hereby recommend a preachers meeting as often as convenient, in every station or circuit, for the instruction and improvement of the preachers in doctrine, &c., and each meeting shall choose its chairman.

LOCAL MINISTERS.

All local ministers that do not belong to the Annual Conference, their cases shall be tried in the Quarterly Conference.

Form of a Marriage Register to be kept by the Quarterly Conference.

Man's name.	Woman's name.	When married.	Where married.	Minister's name.
T. S.	E. S.	18	At the house of	S. W.

Form of a Register of Baptism to be kept by the Quarterly Conference.

Child's name.	When Born.	When Baptised.	Minister's name.	Parent's name
C H.	18	18	D. E.	A. B. C. D.

PREPARED FOR PUBLICATION
BY
HISTORIC PUBLISHING
2017

www.ingramcontent.com/pod-product-compliance
Lightning Source LLC
Chambersburg PA
CBHW050659110426

42739CB00035B/3457